TRUE LOVE
in a World
of False Hope

sex, romance & real people

ROBBIE
CASTLEMAN

D0711653

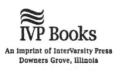

IVP Books
An imprint of InterVarsity Press
Downers Grove, Illinois

InterVarsity Press
P.O. Box 1400, Downers Grove, IL 60515-1426
World Wide Web: www.ivpress.com
E-mail: email@ivpress.com

InterVarsity Press® is the book-publishing division of InterVarsity Christian
Fellowship/USA®, a student movement active on campus at hundreds of universities,
colleges and schools of nursing in the United States of America, and a member
movement of the International Fellowship of Evangelical Students. For information
about local and regional activities, write Public Relations Dept., InterVarsity Christian
Fellowship/USA, 6400 Schroeder Rd., P.O. Box 7895, Madison, WI 53707-7895, or
visit the IVCF website at <www.intervarsity.org>.

All Scripture quotations, unless otherwise indicated, are taken from the Holy Bible,
New International Version®. NIV®. Copyright ©1973, 1978, 1984 by International
Bible Society. Used by permission of Zondervan Publishing House. All rights reserved.

Cover photograph: James Ong/SuperStock

ISBN-10: 0-8308-1958-4
ISBN-13: 978-0-8308-1958-4

Printed in the United States of America ∞

Library of Congress Cataloging-in-Publication Data

Castleman, Robbie, 1949-
    True love in a world of false hope: sex, romance, and real people
    /Robbie Castleman.
        p. cm.
    Includes bibliographical references.
    ISBN 0-8308-1958-4 (paper: alk. paper)
    1. Man-woman relationships. 2. Love. 3. Sex. 4. Interpersonal
relations. I. Title.
    HQ801.C335   1996
    306.7—dc20   96-16813

| P | 22 | 21 | 20 | 19 | 18 | 17 | 16 | 15 | 14 | 13 | 12 | 11 | 10 |
| Y | 19 | 18 | 17 | 16 | 15 | 14 | 13 | 12 | 11 | 10 |

For our parents,
Robert & Luci Fox
Dayton & Lucy Castleman

ACKNOWLEDGMENTS

This book is published during the golden anniversary year of my parents' marriage. Robert and Luci Fox were married on July 6, 1946. I was their second child. My brother, Alan Michael, died of sudden infant death syndrome before I was born. Through this profound sorrow, and through other crises, my parents made it. It was not always easy, but even before their own commitment to Christ, they took their vows of marriage seriously. Both my sister Kellie and I got the idea through their lives that marriage was a good thing. I am grateful to my parents for their model of persistence, repentance, joy and grace.

Breck's parents, Dayton Castleman and Lucy Fletcher Castleman, had a marriage much shorter than my parents or even our own. Married in 1941, Breck's mother died in 1953 when he was eight years old. Although married less than twelve years, Breck's parents created a firm foundation for what a Christian family should be. As a citadel of mission outreach and living for others, the Castlemans honored the Lord. My "father-in-love," as I called Breck's dad, always wore his wedding ring and affectionately recalled his married life with Lucy. "She was really something else, let me tell you!" If such introductions are possible in heaven, I look forward to the day when I will meet the mother of my husband. I think we would have been fine friends.

I also want to thank those friends who kept me thinking and talking and finally writing about this subject. Besides people in the post office, at the gym or in the grocery store, many Inter-Varsity staff and students around the country gave me plenty to think and write about! Thanks to all of you.

I want especially to acknowledge those who prayed for me regularly during the writing of this book. Early in this endeavor I found myself profoundly discouraged. I would have bouts of what felt like a depression. I had no energy for anything, let alone a hard thing—which for me is sitting still to work at the discipline of writing. I felt unfocused and the task seemed impossible. In giving this burden to the Father one morning in prayer, I felt very impressed that what was happening was part of spiritual warfare. I recognized that I was working to help expose one of the longest and best entrenched strongholds of Satan. I believe that the adversary is mightily opposed to the establishment of new Christian homes and families. I think this is one dynamic behind the delay of so many marriages today in the Christian church.

In any event, I secured several people to pray for me three times a week during the year it took to write this book. I would like to thank them within its pages for their faithfulness to this task, their affection for me as their sister in faith, and their love for Breck and me as the Castlemans! So, thanks to Dave and Alice Biggar, Hope and Victor Carrasquilla, Bill and Wendy DePury, Page and Matthew Geske, Antonia Hawkins, Jay and Penni Holt, Kirsten and Chris Kinsley, and Philip and Cindy Swicegood.

And a special thanks to my sons, Rob and Scott, who kept telling me to hurry and get it done so they could read it. I am grateful for their enthusiasm.

And to my lifelong love, Breck, my sweetest appreciation for helping me tell our story—and for giving so much to give away to others.

Prologue:
Edging Toward Eden

People love to talk about sex and relationships. During the time I was writing this book, total strangers would tell me all kinds of things about their lives when they found out I was writing about "personal relationships." One of the postal workers where I mail my manuscripts overheard a comment I made to a friend of mine at another window. The next thing I knew, this man was asking me if I had ever heard of a situation like the one he was in. After he described the situation, I blushed and said that I had not. I also encouraged him to wait to read the book before he made his next move!

Just a few weeks ago, I was minding my own business in a large whirlpool at the health club where my husband and I go. My niece was with me in the pool, and we were commenting on how hot the weather had been this summer. One middle-aged man in the pool said that he was grateful to work at a place with good air conditioning and for a management that allowed shorts and T-shirts. I said, "Yes, I work at home, and it's nice to not have to dress up." I asked him where he worked, and after his answer he responded with a polite question about my line of work.

Now, depending on my mood, I can answer this several ways. If it is a situation where a witness to the gospel looks promising, especially if the conversation is engaged with a college student, I mention that I work for InterVarsity Christian Fellowship in the area of graduate student and faculty ministries. This gives people plenty to respond to, and usually they are curious about what I actually do. If this seems like a remote area of interest to a new acquaintance, I just say, "I am a writer." Since my professional life is divided nearly equally between these two ministries, I feel comfortable answering either way. If I choose this second response, most people will ask, "Oh, what do you write?" When I don't want to talk much or if I am feeling socially awkward, I say, "Oh, stuff—books and articles." That's what I said to this stranger in the whirlpool.

But then my fifteen-year-old niece decided to contribute, "Yes, right now Aunt Robbie is writing a book about sex." What a conversation starter! The three other people in the pool jumped on the topic, and before long two more joined in. Everyone had a story—or two or three—and everyone had a question—or two or three. I was surrounded by people who were in the middle of relational "channel surfing." People were looking for what they craved, but didn't know exactly what that was.

One fellow, on his fourth relationship after two failed marriages, was skeptical that people today could ever really make a good home. "There is too much against us today." A younger man, just past college age, declared, "I will never get married. It's just too hard. I never knew my dad. And my mom did her best, but I wouldn't know how to make it work, not really." An older woman said, "Well, I'm a Christian, and I think God can help a lot." This was nice to hear and I heartily agreed with her, but steered the conversation back to those who were admitting they were clueless. My niece took in every word while people told their stories of frustration, disappointment and hurt. I could hardly believe the reaction myself.

The conversation settled down when one of the men said,

"Well, in your book, just how do you define what love really is?" I smiled and admitted it wasn't original with me, but that "true love was not a noun but a verb that acts like it is 'patient and kind, not jealous or boastful.' " Most of them picked up on the idea that this was from the Bible, and the conversation fizzled slowly from there. Everyone eventually went off to the sauna or steam room, and I sat there with wrinkled fingers, amazed at how desperate people were for a clue about how to have a healthy relationship with someone to love for a lifetime. I saw many people dismiss any notion that learning to love takes some work and that true love is defined by God.

It struck me that we are far from being who we are meant to be as people created as male and female in the image of God. We are far from Eden, the place where we are meant to be. In Eden we could walk with God, and our relationship with our Creator would define and perfectly guide all other relationships. In Eden we could be people, "naked and unshamed." In Eden all would be well. But we are far from Eden, exiles from that ecstasy of perfect belonging and holiness.

I also thought about how, as a Christian, life is a journey home to where we belong. And along the way, those redeemed by Christ become the people we were always meant to be. We are still far from Eden, but, in Christ, we are making our way back to right and holy relationships with God, with others and with ourselves. I believe that the covenant relationship of two believers in marriage contributes a special joy and richness to that journey.

Defining the Ideal

During and after the period of the Enlightenment, when the idea of evolution influenced so much of how we think about life and not just in terms of biology, many people embraced the idea that human beings were just getting better and better. The "ideal person" was somewhere in front of us, in the future.

"Modern" believers, at least in the West, were hopeful and op-
timistic about themselves, the world, each other, and even our
relationship with God.

Two major European wars, the Jewish Holocaust, and the
increase of chaotic and often interethnic violence around the
world have helped usher in a postmodern skepticism about
much of anything getting "better and better." Christians should
be those who recognized this truth all along and who now offer
hope in the middle of the postmodern reality check. G. K. Chesterton was able to do this in the modernity popular in 1908.

In his book *Orthodoxy,* Chesterton makes the eloquent and
typically paradoxical point that the human ideal is not to be
found in looking forward to some person of the future, but in
looking back to Eden, the only place where relationships had
a time of being uncorrupted, holy and right. Chesterton thought
about the insatiable human thirst for the ideal and recognized
the futility of ever achieving this. He then considered the usual
human response to this dilemma and wrote,

We are not altering the real to suit the idea. We are altering
the ideal: it is easier . . . ours is only an age of conservation
because it is an age of complete unbelief. Let beliefs fade fast
and frequently, if you wish institutions to stay the same. . . .
The more the life of the mind is unhinged, the more the
machinery of matter will be left to itself. . . .

As long as the vision of heaven is always changing, the
vision of earth will be exactly the same. . . . How can I answer
if there is no eternal test? . . . A permanent ideal is necessary
. . . it is equally necessary that the vision should be a fixed
vision.

Chesterton reflects on the necessity of an unchangeable ideal
as he thought about his life.

Something seemed to be saying, "My ideal at least is fixed;
for it was fixed before the foundations of the world. My vision
of perfection assuredly cannot be altered; for it is called

Eden. You may alter the place to which you are going; but you cannot alter the place from which you have come. . . . In the upper world hell once rebelled against heaven. But in this world heaven is rebelling against hell . . . a revolution is a restoration. At any instant you may strike a blow for the perfection which none have seen since Adam.

This book is written to encourage such a rebellion. Chesterton makes the point that "man may have had concubines as long as cows have had horns: still they are not a part of him if they are sinful." Too often Christians redefine holiness to fit the time, culture or situation in which they find themselves. We don't do this just to reimagine a new Jesus, excuse sinful sexual practices that give us pleasure, or justify our attempts to love both God and mammon. We also do this to give a religious blessing to the consequences of the Fall. We take God's summary of the curse (Genesis 3:14-16) and tell each other that's the way it is supposed to be. Death, pain, fruitless toil and oppressive and dysfunctional relationships may be fully a part of post-Fall reality, but they are not the way things were supposed to be.

Christians live in the fallen world, but not simply as fallen people. We are people who have been raised with Christ in his resurrection. We are the redeemed. We are on our feet, and our life's journey is to go home and be the people we were always meant to be. Step by step, day by day, we edge our way back to Eden. In this life we will not arrive, but in Christ we know the way. In whirlpools, backyards and university campuses, on buses, from pulpits, in paperbacks and on billboards, Christians point the way home for those who are lost.

Reclaiming God's desire for sexual relationships is a journey toward the holiness of Eden. Holiness, like any truly ultimate ideal, must be an immovable standard. It cannot depend on our historical or cultural context, our socioeconomic bracket, our ethnic background or any other consideration. Holiness must be centered in what is always true about every human being, at all times and in any place.

A colleague of mine, Gary Deddo, works with graduate students and faculty at Princeton through the ministry of InterVarsity. Dr. Deddo summarizes the essentials of our identity in three mandatory relationships that contribute to the "image of God" in the human person. All people are "child and/or parent." We are "male or female." And we are "neighbor—near or far." Issues of living holy lives in an unholy world will center around these three essential relationships.

This book centers around the relationship for which, honestly, the Bible offers us the least complete picture—that of being male and female together in a lifelong loving relationship. I say this because God gives us a most complete picture of who we are to be as human beings in the incarnation of his Son Jesus. In Jesus we get good pictures of what it is like to be a child, how to treat parents and how God is a perfect parent. In Jesus we get great pictures of how to be a good neighbor, as was the sacrificial Samaritan and many others in his stories. But when it comes to gender, our picture is less complete, and Jesus' life is less helpful as a direct model. He was male and not female. He was never married and never in a romantic relationship.

But in the pages of Scripture and in the life of Jesus, we are given much help in what it means to be in relationships with people very different from ourselves, and this can certainly help us in learning to live with and love the opposite sex. The practice of holiness is possible in the relationship between a male and a female. This holiness needs to manifest itself in the two great commissions given by our Creator in Eden: be fruitful and multiply (sexuality, marriage and family) and exercise benevolent dominion over the rest of creation (work, creativity, art, vocation). This book centers around the first commission given in God's perfect and good garden.

I hope this book helps you in your journey as you edge your way toward Eden. It is not a journey we make alone. We travel together, like it or not. And it is not a journey we make without guidance. We travel in the footsteps of many pilgrims who have gone ahead of us. You will find many of their stories in these pages. And as we travel in truth and grace and with the permission of God who alone knows the way home, our Father keeps the light on for us and does not sleep until we arrive where we belong, safe and sound.

1

Hormones
for Holy People

HER: IT IS A DARK and stormy night. Actually, it's three o'clock in the afternoon and only partly cloudy. The weather guy on the radio said, "No chance of rain!" Well, you could have fooled me.

My hair is perfect for once, my blouse is silk, and I have a date. It'll rain. Trust me.

Besides the wet weather, we'll probably go to a place with fried chicken or tomato sauce. Both are destined for the front of the silk.

And what to wear with this blouse? Jeans? Nah, he'll think I'm not treating the date with enough respect. Too casual. Something that matches with a "Dry Clean Only" label? No, too serious. He'll think I'm trying too hard. He'll wonder if I've tried his last name on the back of mine, with or without a hyphen. Actually the hyphenated version doesn't sound too bad . . .

Get a grip, woman! Okay, so back to the closet and something middle-of-the-road.

Okay, the blue thing will do. It's dark enough to minimize any dining or weather disaster. I wish I knew what he was wearing. That would help. Actually, it would help if I was sure he'd remember to show up.

Him

I don't know what good it would do to wax this old thing. Wish I could have borrowed my roommate's car. Oh well, at least she said yes when I asked her out. Should have asked her a month ago, but just didn't want to crash and burn. I almost called her this morning to make sure she remembered, but I thought that might seem a bit too anxious.

When I first pick her up, I will definitely open the car door for her. Then, when we get to the restaurant, I'll go around the back of the car slowly enough to see if she opens her own door. If she waits, then okay. I'll know what she likes. I wish I had time to wax the car, but it'll probably rain anyway. But that might be good. If I have the only umbrella, she will automatically wait for me to come around and open her door.

Where to eat? I can't afford seafood or steak. I wish payday was this week. I guess we'll try that new Italian place. Who doesn't like spaghetti? And the place just opened. So hopefully no old memories of some Mr. Perfect to compete with.

Get a grip, man! Compete for what? This is just a date. What should I wear? Whatever's clean, I guess. Maybe I should have done laundry instead of washing this heap.

Getting a Grip

Sexuality is part of God's created goodness. Like all the physically experienced gifts of our Creator, its appetite can be enjoyed by obedience or abused by disobedience. We can drink to satisfy our thirst or "be drunk with wine to excess." We can eat to energize our lives or become gluttonous or anorexic to put our lives in danger. We can acknowledge and celebrate our sexuality within the benevolent perimeters of God's will or we can impose our own will and be disobedient. This disobedience can be expressed from promiscuity to the denial of any expression of sexuality.

We journey toward Eden as sexual people. Unlike food and drink, full sexual expression is not a requirement of physical survival. But like eating and drinking, sexuality must be acknowledged as part of God's design for us. Budget, personal taste and health may prohibit certain foods or beverages for an individual, but the person would still eat and drink. Singleness prohibits sexual intercourse (as well as physical expression that explicitly prepares the body for intercourse), but being single does not mandate a blanket denial of every sexual feeling or expression.

Dating can be an arena of better understanding and wisely expressing personal sexuality. This arena is encircled by the benevolent boundaries of God's design and perfect wisdom. These boundaries are *benevolent* because God is good and desires good for his children. Sexuality is designed and desired for us by God. It is not given to be denied. Our sexuality is not designed to be an unredeemable frustration, temptation or sin. Certain expressions and feelings of sexuality can be frustrating, tempting and sinful, but even in singleness this is not God's purpose nor the way things have to be.

Hormones Are Not the Invention of the Evil One

The devil did not invent hormones; they are part of our God-created humanity. There is a trend among some Christians to prohibit *any* expression of sexuality by unmarried people. Recently a married friend commented that any feelings of "sensuality" even *within* marriage were prohibited. In trying to clarify what was meant by "sensuality," he included any feelings of bodily desire for another—even a marriage partner. Sexual desire was considered sinful. I disagree. Sexual desire is a human appetite given by God *before* the rebellion in Eden.

In fact, the sequence of blessing and command in Genesis 1:27–31 is good to note. The Creator's first command is "be fruitful and increase in number." This is followed by "rule" over the creation. And this is followed by God's generous provision of food. God's design for us in the very beginning included making families, working to care for the creation and enjoying his provision for earthly life. All these things were exercised within the arena of holiness before the rebellion of our human parents, and God summarized his desire and design as "very good."

All these very good things were directly corrupted by rebellion. Genesis 3:16–19 records that human reproduction will include pain, male-female relationships will be prone to lust and exploitation, once-joyful work will be toilsome and its results unpredictable in providing food. God's people were not told to stop eating, working or having sex. We were told that all these things would be more difficult and require ultimate redemption. This redemption is not completed until the resurrection of our bodies (Romans 8:19–23). Until then, Christians recognize the potential for sin in all these things and learn to live obediently. And while we learn, we trust in a Savior greater than our sin, a Redeemer greater than our rebellion. We believe that nothing in all of fallen creation will be able to separate us from the love of God in the Savior and Redeemer, Christ Jesus (Romans 8:37–39).

Delay Is Not Denial

There are times to delay work. A good vacation can make one a better worker. There are times to delay food. Fasting often precedes an especially appreciated meal or a powerful prayer time. There are times to delay expressions of sexuality. Abstinence and less exclusive delays of sexuality can create an appetite for sexual expression that honors God's original desire.

To delay can honor God's opinion that work, food and sex

are very good. To "deny" any of these in a way that excludes them from the possibility of holiness dishonors God's design and intention for our lives.

Delay takes sexuality seriously. To delay sexual expression creates time to confront and appreciate the power of the sexual appetite. Delay is not denial. Too many people do not take their sexuality seriously enough. They deny sexual feelings, dismiss temptation, ignore internal warnings and overspiritualize personal attraction to the opposite sex. People in the midst of denial can get blind-sided by something they refused to see.

Actually, denial doesn't take the Savior seriously enough. Sexuality is a part of God's original design for human beings, and it doesn't make him nervous. It may sound funny to think of God as "nervous," but many of us do. We may know this is not true theologically, but often in day-to-day living we treat God's faithfulness to us as fickle—we feel like we live on the edge of rejection. The nervousness we feel is projected onto God the Father. We visualize him like an earthly father, albeit a *good* earthly father, who is a bundle of nerves until we "come home safely."

Scripture tells us that we are entrusted by Christ Jesus to our good heavenly Father, who is able to keep us for himself until the day of our reunion. (John 17:11, 15; 2 Timothy 1:12; Titus 2:14; Jude 24). Our God is able to keep us. To deny our sexuality is to tell ourselves that it is a part of us that doesn't need to be "kept" by the Father—it is somehow immune. To acknowledge our sexuality is to take its power seriously, and this helps create a dependence on our good Father for his keeping and care.

God is not nervous about the sexual desires and power of our humanity. God *is* faithful, watchful, full of guidance and able to keep us until we are safely home as his redeemed people.

Living by Faith, Not Fraud
In the meantime we can live by faith. We can live with con-

fidence in God's goodness.

Many Christians don't experience the security of this relationship with God. The Creator knows everything there is to know about us, and freely chooses to love us. God calls us to live honest lives of learning what it means to walk by faith. He loves who we are and eagerly sent the Holy Spirit to be our counselor, guide and comforter. The Lord is faithful, and the good work he began in us will be completed (Philippians 1:6). He is saddened by sin, but he is not surprised by it.

So we learn to live by faith, not by fraud. In a recent movie a character portrayed by Debra Winger was bemoaning the fact that she never really got to know herself: "I don't know who I am. I was always reinventing myself for every new relationship." Learning to be who we are with others is an exercise of learning to trust God to be the redeemer of our sin, the healer of our brokenness and the foundational security of our lives. Christians need not reinvent themselves for relationships. We can risk being known and loved (or not loved) by others because we are known and loved for sure by God.

We need to become who we are in Christ. And we need to be who we are in fact with other people. Letting people know us, being honest about our feelings and fears, is one way to live by faith. If honest living is difficult generally, it is more difficult in relationships with a romantic potential. We can be so dishonest in even the most casual of friendships. If Eden is not our destination, it is hard to know in which direction to head. We can worry over the simplest of evenings.

To Date or Not to Date, This Is the Question

If you are like many, the potential for success or disaster in a first date with someone is enough to preoccupy and distract a usually focused mind. The possibilities of continuing a dating relationship can be enough to call the whole thing off or never get started.

The latter choice is often the advice given to Christians who want to date. "Don't date" is frequently coupled with an admonition about trusting God, not getting distracted, or with questions about being "ready" for a serious romantic relationship. There are certainly reasons not to date, but these are not necessarily right reasons. "Don't date" *is* good advice if the intended date is with someone who is not a Christian. You can do plenty of good things with and for friends who are not Christians. Dating is not one of them.

Dating does imply an interest in a person that has romantic potential, even a vague or distant potential. We need to be honest about that with ourselves. That potential, if we are to be faithful followers of Jesus Christ, necessarily excludes any risk of romance with a person who does not share the very faith that defines who we are.

Can dating help us in our journey toward Eden? What about dating and "trusting God"? What about dating and "getting distracted"? What about dating and knowing what it means to be "ready" for true romance?

Dating can be a way to trust God. Exploring the lifelong possibilities with a friend can be a tremendous exercise of faith. In getting to know someone, you get to know yourself better. Learning to trust God with new feelings, physical temptations, personal comfort zones and the opposite sex can help make your relationship with God more honest. This isn't a reason to date, but it does address blanket prohibitions against doing so.

Dating can be distracting, but it doesn't have to be. It is good to be clear about the kind of distraction under consideration. Is it mental and emotional, just-can't-concentrate distraction? These can be signs of an infatuation with the unknowns about a situation or person. Often, as an unknown becomes known, distracting and preoccupying tendencies give way to a greater focused creativity and increased energy. This can happen when two people who are dating discover common interests and are surprised to find similar experiences. This same kind of creativity and energy can be experienced when a scholar understands something that was once baffling. An athlete who finally learns to hit a curve ball will be more confident in the batter's box facing an unknown pitcher.

Or is the admonition not to date a caution that it can distract from one's relationship with God? It is all too easy to get distracted from disciplines that encourage a healthy personal relationship with God, his people and his work. Dating is hardly the only culprit that can foster such distraction. Many things, including food, physical fitness, hobbies and even children, can distract from the disciplines and duties of the Christian life. But we don't give them up. We shouldn't give them up. By faith, and with reliance on the Spirit's manifestation of self-control, we can give proper place and time to these delights. This can include dating. All the pleasures of life are given by God for our good. We can corrupt them. Or we can learn to celebrate them with holiness and joy.

What about "being ready" before a dating relationship? Ready for what? Many times the advice against dating is a well-intended attempt to protect another from emotional injury, the vulnerability of increasing relational intimacy or the temptation of sexual lust. This implies having an impenetrable shield against the harsh realities of life. But will we ever be that ready? Christians are called to "walk by faith, not by sight." We cannot live by faith and eliminate life's unpredictable emotions, vulnerabilities or temptations. We can learn to trust God with the risks and realities of life that are part of the human condition. We can learn how to be wise and not foolish about those risks and realities. We can learn, during times when emotional injury, relational vulnerability and temptation are real, that God is the greater reality.

There may be times when dating is an unwise risk. There are times for concentrated efforts to sort out feelings, identify weaknesses, acknowledge personal tendencies and preferences, get over disappointments and gain a better understanding of family patterns that influence how you function in relationships. But these times never finish the job. None of us are ever completely ready for an intimate relationship. We never know enough to know who we are. Even with the love of 1 Corinthians 13, we "see but a poor reflection" of ourselves, others or our God.

No one is ever completely ready for life. We are never completely in control. This is exactly the situation that makes for a life of faith. It also makes for a life that is more uncomfortable and yet more complete with a community of companions. Someday this may mean committing to a lifelong marriage relationship with a special companion of the opposite sex. God recognized in our perfect beginning that it was "not good for the man to be alone." He has never changed his mind. It is risky, but it is also right. Dating isn't the only way to discover if a friend can be a lifelong companion. It can, however, be one way to do just that. And accepting our sexuality can be one way God introduces us to his original design for our lives.

Human sexuality is redeemable. The denial of human sexuality is a rejection of the Redeemer's power to overcome all the consequences and curses of the Fall. In the power of the resurrection, believers can "do all things" to God's glory. In Christ Jesus we can *be* the working, eating and sexual human beings God called "very good." In Christ Jesus, the dark and stormy nights of dating can be transformed into fair-weather days of discovery and delight.

2

Sex &
a Bad-Hair Day

BECOMING FRIENDS with our sexuality can be a problem because we often think of our body as the enemy. We don't like the way we look. How our bodies seem to behave is a mystery at times. A bad-hair day, hormones and Aunt Hilda's or Uncle Hank's nose can all make your body a threat to who you think you are deep down, or who you really want to be. One look in the mirror can make us wonder what God, or anyone else, could possibly love.

It's amazing how many blurry snapshots I have of people who are trying to avoid having their picture taken! "I look awful!" is the common protest from very ordinary-looking women. The ordinary-looking guys just tend to duck, turn away or make a face.

Not many of these blurry folks look awful at all. They look like who they are. Now, not many would end up on the cover of *GQ* or *Glamour*, but I just want these friends to end up looking like themselves in my photo album.

Family photo opportunities aren't much better.

My grandmother celebrated her ninety-fifth birthday last year, and all of her living children, all of her grandchildren and nearly all of her great-grandchildren gathered to wish her well. As the oldest grandchild (and the one to remember camera and film), I coordinated all the picture-taking. I was exhausted by the amount of cajoling it took to take pictures that no one wanted to pose for. A whole family that "just looked awful"— fixing hair, smoothing clothes, sucking in tummies, hiding behind another cousin and generally acting like we all do. None of us liked how we looked, and we looked just like we always do. (And of course everyone wanted copies of the pictures when it was all over!)

Lots of people don't like how they look. We have a love-hate relationship with our bodies. We like clear skin, the right weight for our height, clothes that flatter and hair that cooperates. We will spend money and take time to have the skin, figure, wardrobe and hairstyle we want. But we are seldom satisfied with the results of our efforts. We could always look better. Someone else always looks better. This someone may be a roommate or a stranger, someone on the cover of a magazine or your rival sibling. This someone may be the composite drawing of our most perfect self. *If I could afford a Soloflex. If I had the time. If I had the clothes. If I didn't have Aunt Hilda's nose. If . . .*

Friends, family and the famous—none of us are satisfied. Just this morning I read in the newspaper that actress Demi Moore would appear completely nude on a magazine cover for the *fourth time!* You think one could assume Ms. Moore is a physically self-confident and satisfied person. Wrong. My hometown paper quotes her listing a "slew of perceived flaws" in *Rolling Stone* magazine. "Eyes too small . . . I'm kind of a plain Jane. I don't have a good smile, I have no waist . . ." Think what she could hide with clothes!

Body and Soul, Human Unity

Christians often share this same desire and discontent, if not the unique photo-op of Demi Moore. Most of my blurry photos are of brothers and sisters in the Christian family. On top of this same desire and discontent, Christians often verbally deny that the body matters at all. "It's the spirit that counts." Or "It's what's inside that matters."

True, but Christian theology rooted in the incarnation of Jesus Christ asserts that the spiritual side of life is not *all* that counts. In fact Christianity, rooted in good Hebrew tradition, refuses to separate life into "sides." There is no "body" side opposing the "spiritual" side. Both body and soul are created things. They are connected and linked. The Hebrew word for "person" or "self" or "soul" is the same word used for "body," "flesh" or "corpse." The body and soul are a unity. We travel toward Eden as people with real bodies and souls.

Bethlehem and Our Bodies

The incarnation of Jesus, God in human flesh, brought redemption to the human person—body and soul. God did not reject the human body even for his own Son. He was conceived by the Spirit in the womb of a young Jewish virgin. He was born like other infants, grew like other toddlers, learned like other children and matured like other men. Jesus lived among us without sin as God and with a body as a human being.

The human body is not the "prison of the soul," as some Greek philosophers taught. The body is the "temple of the Holy Spirit," according to the Word of God (1 Corinthians 6:19). I heard a five-year-old tell her mother that lightning was "God taking my picture." The five-year-old may have flunked science, but her theology was good. God loves the human body. He is not estranged from our humanity. He is not frustrated with his physical creation. In fact, God does not even want us to be disembodied after death.

Everlasting life isn't bodiless. The redeemed will not be disembodied ghosts. Scripture promises a resurrected body like that of the Lord Jesus, imperishable and immortal (1 Corinthians 15:50-54). Transformed, but real. Jesus said after his resurrection, "Look at my hands and my feet. It is I myself! Touch me and see; a ghost does not have flesh and bones, as you see I have" (Luke 24:39). Jesus promises to perfect our bodies in the prototype of his own resurrected body. Even in heaven our bodies will not be a prison but a part of our personhood.

License or Loathing

When we consider our bodies as "the enemy" to our best selves, we can create an imbalance in the way we view the spiritual side of our lives. When the body is viewed as disconnected from the soul, two basic tendencies in behavior generally result. These behaviors are direct opposites. Some people tend to deny the real importance of the body by an attitude that says, "The body doesn't really matter, so what the body does doesn't really matter." This leads to an anything-goes mentality and develops into physical licentiousness. This is the person who says, "I just can't help it! This is the way we're made, so who cares?" Indulging the body's appetite for sex, food, drink or drug-enhanced sensual experiences without regard for health or physical consequences is one response to buying into a false body-soul dichotomy.

The other response is not promiscuity but punishment. Not licentiousness but loathing is another way of seeing the body as an enemy. Eating disorders (anorexia and bulimia are the more obvious examples), chronic sleep deprivation, body mutilation and extremes in exercise can all be ways of attempting to punish the body—treating it as the enemy. Instead of indulging the body because it really doesn't matter, the body is denied because it really doesn't count.

In regard to sexual expression, these two responses to the

body-as-enemy can be more subtle. Indulgence can sound like, "But I really love her/him, and we are planning to get married, so what does it really matter if we sleep together now?" This is saying that bodily sexual expression has little or nothing to do with what really matters inside—the love felt between two people. But it does matter. "Inside" love is very much connected to "outside" expressions of that love. The degree of heartbreak when a relationship ends is directly affected by the degree of physical intimacy shared in the relationship.

Safer Sex?
A short time ago I met with a college student who ended a six-month dating relationship. As she sorted through her feelings, one of the things she recognized was the wisdom both she and the young man exercised to limit physical expressions of affection while they were dating. "There could be so much more to regret," she confessed, "if we had not agreed to keep our physical expressions in step with our emotional commitment."

Both sides—body and soul—matter. "Safer Sex" is the promotional motto for condom use on college campuses, but there is a part of sexual reality that is ignored. You can't put a condom on your heart. Our outside conduct affects our inside condition. The human person is an undivided body-soul. Indulgence and denial are both unhealthy.

This young couple did not deny their sexuality; they took their sexual feelings seriously. Neither did they indulge their sexual feelings as a man and a woman. They controlled their appetite, and as a consequence of this relationship they both know better what kind of person they will date next time. Self-control can create a healthy appetite. An indulgent sexual response leads to regret, and like junk food eaten before a well-prepared dinner, it can kill a healthy appetite.

The second response to the body-as-enemy is even more subtle and can sound more sanctified. Instead of indulging the sexual appetite, a person tries to function as a sexual "eunuch" without a ministry call that demands this sacrifice. This denial of the sexual appetite can sound like "I don't ever want to get married!" Or "Relationships are so messy. I'm better off just by myself." Self-isolating statements can be expressions of self-loathing. "I don't like myself, and no one else ever will either."

People can use spiteful language to deny sexual longings. "All men are scum, and I don't need anybody." "All women are manipulative liars, and I'll never trust one." Hostility can be an attempt to hide feelings that cause fear or create discomfort. Hateful expressions can be attempts to mask a suspicion that certain situations can be deeply threatening. Feelings of physical sexuality can be confusing to people who view the body as a threat to their sense of well-being.

People can use spiritual language to deny the sexual appetite. "I don't need anybody; Jesus keeps me company." "Embracing my singleness has made me a better person." The possible truth in such expressions is probably the most difficult to discern because both of these statements can be said out of real faith, not sexual denial and fear.

Don't misunderstand what I am trying to expose here. There is a fraudulent spirituality that denies the God-created goodness of the body that makes us sexual people. Sometimes this fraud camouflages itself in a superspirituality that denies our humanity.

God does not begrudge us our humanity. He recognizes our basic need for companionship and belonging. The family was God's idea, and he has never changed his mind. I am not saying that singleness is inherently wrong or that a relationship with Jesus is in anyway inadequate. What I am saying is that a tendency to sanctify singleness needs to be examined. The Creator said being "alone" is not good for us (Genesis 2:18), and God has never changed his mind. The increasing reticence of many Christians to marry is not born from an obedience to a call to kingdom work that demands singleness, but from a poor theology that denies the created goodness of the sexual relationship and seeks to divide body and soul.

Our churches are filled with lonely people who are unwilling to trust God with their sexuality. For the one caught in this body-as-enemy attitude, it is only a small step to see another's body as an even greater threat. Many think the opposite sex isn't just opposite, it's alien. So the unknowns are just too great to risk such vulnerability. Of course, most believers will say the faith they lack is not in the Creator, but in themselves or in others. The truth is, though, that many don't believe that God cares as much for the body as he does for the soul. But God sees no distinction; he cares for the whole person.

The Single's Dilemma

Certainly, people give other reasons for a hesitancy to commit themselves to intimate relationships. A lack of healthy role models is a significant one. Many young people today come from homes—marked by divorce, violence, dysfunctionality and hostility—that discourage them from believing that marriage is desirable. Little evidence of courtesy, let alone affection, is seen in many homes. There is a real lack of models of positive relationships within families. So single people either have no serious desire to risk attempting a lifelong relationship or have no clear idea of how to take even the first step.

There is also the dynamic of cultural correctness and church traditions. Men and women get all sorts of signals and outright mandates today about what is the "right" thing to do or not to do—what the right attitude is to not be "sexist." But then the church often urges very different values and behaviors. In the world, men and women are expected to be equal in initiating relationships, contacts, projects and the like. In the church, to a great extent, the initiative in a dating relationship is expected of the male.

And in many churches singles are isolated by activities and programs and schedules from the families and couples that could provide healthy and positive role models for marriage. "Singles" worship, Sunday schools, programs, activities, ministries—even habits of sitting in a certain place in the sanctuary—can work to isolate young people from the very help they need in the area of relationships. Compound this with the unspoken pressures many singles groups create to "find someone," and the results can be an entrenched hopelessness.

Another reason that a commitment to marriage is delayed or denied is an inflated idea of life's necessities. Not only young people but also their parents put things before a relationship. In less sanctified terms, the reluctance to marry, or prolonged delay in marrying, may be the result of worldliness or selfishness. A down payment on a house, dining-room furniture, a better car or even a diploma is not a prerequisite to a good relationship. Choosing to live more simply can be an act of faith and a declaration of love.

I have had many conversations with young dating couples whose relationship has grown more physically intimate than they desired. Such intimacy is often a real reflection of their emotional commitment to each other. They truly love each other. They want to get married, but . . . Sometimes this "but" has to do with finishing school. I remind them that God is more concerned with their relationship and their holiness as his people than he is about the date on their diplomas. Very often marriage simplifies the stress-filled schedules of single people. My point here is not that getting married is the solution for every stressed-out dating couple. My point is that "finishing school" is often an unexamined excuse for not marrying that too often leads to sexual sin and emotional scars that can destroy a potentially lifelong and satisfying relationship.

Hollywood, Not Holiness

Sadly, this "but" can also stem from expectations of life's needs grown in the soil of Hollywood, not holiness. Many young people today cannot imagine being married without a ring that everyone will notice and a wedding that everyone will talk about. The wedding becomes a greater focus of attention than the marriage. My husband, who is a pastor, has often commented that people spend more time planning for a thirty-minute wedding than preparing for thirty years of marriage. The image of love becomes more important than the substance of love.

It is not uncommon to set a wedding date according to the availability of a reception site rather than the needs of the relationship itself. Too many relationships are significantly hurt or ruined altogether by the stress, tension and compromise experienced because the consumer culture has defined the needs for God's people. And parents, Christian or not, frequently promote these same unexamined expectations for their children. No wonder the body and soul seem at war.

Sexuality is part of our essential personhood. God has not made our bodies to be the prisons of our souls. He does not want our bodies to be a threat to our relationships. There are many ways that we send ourselves to war against ourselves. Too often we don't accept ourselves, body and soul, and so we don't love ourselves or each other very wisely or well.

Accepting our bodies as God's gift and the dwelling place of his Spirit can help us make better choices in being kind to this physical treasure. Valuing our bodies and recognizing its appetites as God-given can enhance the Spirit's fruit of self-control in our lives. This is not a self-control that denies the self, but a self-control that honors the sexual appetite, refuses the junk food of promiscuity or punishment, and creates a place to be loved and not alone.

3

Sex Ed,
Jimmy Kaye & KYEOJ

I WAS A LATE BLOOMER. In junior high I was just a skinny little kid who longed for the day I could wear a bra. It was so cool and grown up to see a girl's bra strap through the back of her blouse. All the cheerleaders had this mark of distinction. It wasn't until ninth grade that I "had enough" to justify this sartorial splendor. I remember the inaugural day very well—I got thrown in the shower for it after gym class by my sensitive friends. So you can understand when I say that I am sympathetic about love-hate relationships concerning the body.

In those days sex was pretty much a muddled mystery confined to the mature lives of "bad girls." My mother's well-meaning talk assumed a whole lot. The birds-and-bees education I heard as a twelve-year-old (probably on a day I talked about a cute boy) went like this:

Now, Robbie, let me just tell you one thing. You are going to like boys. Just remember, you are going to want it. But don't forget, the boy just zips up his pants and goes home. The girl pays the price and is left with a loaf in the oven.

I do not lie. This verbatim parental lecture has been confirmed by my sister. She got the same one on a similar occasion. In fact, when I telephoned my sister to verify this recollection, she told me that her daughter, my niece, had received a letter from our mom sharing this same enigmatic advice when she was "old enough." My sister added that Mom's letter included the revelation that "this was what my Grandmother Ava told me, what I told your Aunt Robbie and your mother."

This cross-generational advice may be inadequate in spots (I remember thinking, *Want what?*), but it did communicate two valuable pieces of reliable truth. One, whatever this desire was, it was definitely desirable. And two, boys and girls have a very different experience with "it." Of course I knew that something sexual was being referred to. But for more information on mature subjects, I called my most buxom girlfriend, Jimmy Kaye.

Jimmy Kaye filled me in on the details. I remember the night well. We were having a twosome sleepover. It was really late, really dark, and we were talking on the rollaway bed out on our patio. This was the best place to sleep on a hot summer night in Nevada. I told Jimmy Kaye what my mother had said, and asked her, "What exactly is it that I will want?"

Jimmy Kaye told me. I was horrified. "He does what?!" Jimmy Kaye, in her virginal but mature confidence, reassured me that this was the way things were done.

I was fascinated and began to look at boys in a whole new way. I wondered which ones knew this information. And when I heard that a ninth-grader got "left with a loaf in the oven," I remember being amazed that it must all really be true.

The Awe Factor
My sex education may have lacked charts and graphs for quite a while, but it did not lack for awe. I was struck with the "fear of the fact," just as believers are struck with the "fear of the

Lord." Scripture tells us this reverential awe is the "beginning of wisdom." My mother did communicate some wisdom if not much information. I did end up liking boys. And a longing for intimacy surely did develop. But my sense of awe slowed me down, made me thoughtful, and my husband married a virgin.

It wasn't until I was nineteen years old that this awe-inspired self-restraint was undergirded by the wisdom of God's instruction in Scripture. I was a junior in college when I became a Christian. I was in nursing school, so I understood all the sexual anatomy and physiology correctly, but it wasn't until I met my Creator that I understood my sense of self-restraint as kind and actually purposeful. I began to understand that sex was awesome because it involved all of who I am. And who I am is a beloved child of my heavenly Father who wants the best for me.

My mom's advice about sex was her way of wanting the best for me. She and Dad loved me, and probably the best sex-education they offered came in their love for each other. Even before the gospel's redemption of my family, there was a lot of goodness and grace in our home.

I remember my parents as affectionate and even frisky at times. As a child I couldn't appreciate how their playful flirting in the car or kitchen gave me a sense that marriage was good, even fun. They hugged and kissed each other, not just their daughters. My sister Kellie and I knew they were unseen lovers.

This playful legacy has marked my own marriage. Our sons know their dad and I are in love with each other. They have caught us kissing in the kitchen, seen us snuggle on the couch, heard us say words of endearment. When they were still young boys, before their first basketball camp, my husband and I had the "talk" with them. I did not pass along Great-Grandmother Ava's original version, but I did try to instill that same sense of awe. In adolescence our sons were curious about our sex life, and asked us lots of questions. Some we've answered.

Some we've said, "You'll find out."

Advice and awe. Wise parents provide both for their children. Wise children listen, learn and remember. Truly blessed children look and see a life of love in the relationship of their parents. Edging toward Eden as a family can make the journey a true *holiday.*

Not Magic, But Just Right

A lot of good sex education begins with the words "I remember the day I met your father." My sons heard our story many, many times and even asked us to tell their friends. I remember the place, the time and the day. But at first I couldn't remember his name.

It was New Orleans. St. Charles Avenue. June 24, 1971. It was hot, humid, and I was hungry. Casual introductions were made among the group of friends who met in front of Kolb's German restaurant. Fine. Let's eat. That guy with the crinkly blue eyes, what was his name? Brett? Brent? I was corrected. Breck. Like the shampoo. Now, what do I want to eat? Eating German food in Cajun-French-Creole-Seafood New Orleans should have been a clue that something different was about to happen.

What was different was the rest of my life. The summer job I'd taken as a nurse at a summer boys' camp turned into a permanent reassignment geographically as well as professionally. But on that hot summer's night in June all I knew was that this Presbyterian youth pastor was a nice guy and that New Orleans was like no place I'd ever been. The group of us listened to jazz at Preservation Hall, ate beignets at the Café du Monde and walked the French Quarter streets. I remember the first time I saw the Mississippi River. I scampered down the levee and put my foot in the water. I never thought I'd see the river again, but I ended up living within fourteen blocks of the Mississippi for the next sixteen years.

That June night was nice, but it wasn't magic. One thing

about lifelong love is that it starts somewhere and sometime when we aren't aware of it. Movies like *Sleepless in Seattle* and other works of Hollywood fiction make it seem like love comes as sudden and magical insight. (Hollywood fiction also portrays intercourse as instantly easy and never awkward.) Sometimes Christians are looking for the same magic in more sanctified terms. It's easy to get more caught up in creating the "right chemistry" than being in a "right relationship" with whomever you are with. Learning to let God be on the lookout, and keeping our eyes on Jesus is no small work of obedience—especially when you're lonely.

KYEOJ

I remember how hard it was to learn to trust the Lord when I was lonely and single. As a young Christian I wanted to just be myself and let God take care of me. Easier desired than done, right? I had enough game playing and flirting in my high-school and early college life. After my conversion, I discovered that habits of the culture are hard to break. It helped to have a friend who shared the same struggle. My friend Alice, who came to know Christ just about the same time I did, was prone to flirt and play games with guys in the fellowship just like I did.

It was so easy to slip into saying the "like-me" things instead of replying with an honest response. Or to feign an interest in ideas or activities that really didn't interest us. Or to dress in such a way to catch someone's eye. We prayed together about our tendencies to be dishonest about ourselves—our feelings, desires, ideas, intelligence and preferences—just to try to interest a guy. Alice and I prayed together about our sinful and self-centered patterns of behavior, and we came up with the idea to "KYEOJ."

"KYEOJ" (pronounced KEY-aw-j) was our acronym for "Keep Your Eyes On Jesus." It was pretty simple, but it sure helped us take our first baby steps toward Eden. In a group situation where we would catch each other doing the worldly flirt thing, we'd mumble to each other, "KYEOJ." We then had to recognize our behavior and revise our conversation or attitude. We even had small coins made with "KYEOJ" on them to carry with us. We made them in a machine outside the Disneyland attraction "Pirates of the Caribbean." Our college fellowship had gone to Southern California for a fun time, and we really found ourselves tempted time and again during this trip. We needed all the help we could get. This acronym and accountability helped us unlearn a worldly pattern of behavior. Frankly, "KYEOJ" was a constant call to repentance.

We learned that "KYEOJ-ing" worked. When Alice met Jim and when I met Breck, it was the Lord who had to draw our attention to these godly men. And when Jim met Alice and Breck met Robbie, they met who we really were, not someone else we were trying to be. You see, flirting creates a caricature that you can't keep up for too many years let alone a lifetime. Many divorces are the product of flirting-fatigue—even among Christians! One person or both in the relationship just gets tired of being someone they aren't. Someone discovers they don't really love the person they are married to because they never knew the real person they married.

Real Love

Alice and I wanted to be loved. But we wanted to be loved for who we really were—young Christians who longed to be mature disciples of Jesus. So we worked on it. We held each other accountable. We "KYEOJ-ed." And on that hot June night, I met a man who would prove to be my lifelong love. I just didn't know it. Breck met a woman that night who scampered down the levee to put her foot in the Mississippi River at midnight. This behavior was definitely "me," and definitely stupid. No one should put their foot in this river! Breck met a woman who went bonkers over jazz at Preservation Hall, started a pow-dered-sugar fight at Café du Monde and wanted to talk about Reformed theology until four in the morning.

I met a man who was careful about everything he did and said. Not cautious, just careful. He was thoughtful and mature in his faith. I learned that his dad was a pastor and his mom had been a missionary in China. I learned he wouldn't start a powdered-sugar fight, but he'd join in! He warned me not to go down the levee and put my foot in the water, but he let me learn my own lesson. He didn't go bonkers over jazz at Pres-ervation Hall, but he thoroughly enjoyed it. And he loved to talk about the faith until four in the morning.

We didn't know it that night, but we had met who we needed in our lives. I met someone who was a stable, steady saint. He met someone who was a spontaneous, spark-plug saint. Be-tween us, we're pretty balanced. We didn't know that night how good we would be for each other. But the Lord did. Keep-ing our eyes on Jesus eventually gave us eyes for each other. And edging toward Eden together has been a joy.

True Love

A desire for each other grew. By the end of that summer, we realized this was the real thing, and honest sexual temptation became part of the battle to "KYEOJ"! Saints aren't immune from temptations, but they do have the reason and the re-sources to resist them. I have found that Christians are often surprised by sexual temptation—as if they should not be fully subject to this human appetite.

Hormones don't know if they are Christian or not. Christians, however, do know what to do about human and hormonal temptation. Keep your eyes on Jesus and your hands to your-self! I didn't make up an acronym for that, but Breck and I did set some guidelines for our dating conduct. We also set a date for our wedding.

Breck and I found in each other someone we were unusually comfortable with. At the time I thought of him as a person who made me feel more comfortable with being me. Breck described it in terms of ice cream. I was just the right "flavor"—just what he had a "taste" for. He told me that on a lonely night during seminary he had written a bit of prose about "love and the 31 flavors of Baskin-Robbins ice cream." I was simply the thirty-second flavor. He found me satisfying as a person. Not perfect, just satisfying. Not magic, just right.

Movies like *Sleepless in Seattle* and other Hollywood works of fiction can lead one to believe that there is a one-in-a-million chance of meeting just the right person. There are a lot of lonely Christians who have believed this romantic roulette. It's just not like that. Falling in love is a lot like faith. You don't really know how it will be when you take that step of faith, but you know who orders the step. Not everything clicks, falls into place or is perfect. Good theology, as well as honest experience, tells you that the person you fall in love with is a sinner. Falling in love is an act of faith. I doubt the theory that there is just one person (or job or place to live) "right" for each of us. I do believe that God calls us to an act of faith in a relationship that we find enhancing our discipleship, edging us in the right direction—toward Eden.

Some of you may want to ask me, "Just how do you *know for sure* when it's true love?" I have to say honestly, you don't know for sure before the first step of obedience. You don't really know how sweet the marvelous light is when you are still in darkness. Faith has its risks. Faith is never foolish, but faith is required when all the questions aren't answered. God can be trusted to inform our faith, guide our love and help our obedience.

Our heavenly Father is more like my mother than I care to admit sometimes. He doesn't give me all the information I want, but he offers me enigmatic wisdom that requires me to trust and have faith in him as a perfect parent.

I can offer a little more information, but I can't resolve the mystery. Falling in love is like the Grand Canyon. You haven't seen it until you've been there—no matter how many pictures you see, or brochures or books you read. And like the Grand Canyon, love is worth the journey. It's like nothing you've ever seen before.

4

Ain't Love Grand?

THE GRAND CANYON, as awe-inspiring as it is today, didn't begin so grandly. The first trickle of the Colorado River gave no hint to what it would carve out in time. Today's Grand Canyon tourists can hike or take a mule-train ride to the bottom of the canyon, in places more than a mile below the canyon's rim. The width of the canyon today ranges from four to eighteen miles, and the length from its beginnings in the Little Colorado River to Lake Meade is 217 miles.

The river bed was pretty simple in the beginning. Water and rock. Tourists today find it much the same at the bottom. Water and rock. But what a view! If we had seen the first Colorado River bed, it would have been hard to believe that something so spectacular could begin from such simple beginnings.

Lifelong romantic love, like the Grand Canyon, usually begins with an unobtrusive trickle—a friendship that creates a special niche in your heart. Now, not all rivers create the Grand Canyon, and not all opposite-sex friendships end in the lifelong love of marriage. But the latter happens, and it happens far more often than rivers create a grand geographical niche in the earth's surface.

The bedrock of a grand marriage is friendship. A good marriage may commence after a short friendship or a lengthy friendship, but it always needs to begin with a friend. A male-female friendship may continue as a platonic relationship, but it is still a relationship between a person who is male and a person who is female. Romantic expressions of sexuality are excluded in a platonic relationship, but being a friend does not make a person sexually neutral. Every human being is either male or female. Our gender is a significant part of who we are.

Gender and the "Opposite" Sex

Gender differences do not make the sexes "opposite," although we use the term, but the distinctions of sexuality between the genders do make us "other." Men and women tend to have distinctive angles for viewing the world, communicating within the world and relating to others in the world. No wonder men and women often say to each other, "What in the world do you mean?" Or "Why in the world would you do that?" Even when the confusion is unspoken, the sentiment is common.

You can observe notable behavioral differences between the sexes in our culture. None of these are certain or set within a person, but a general tendency can exist in many people. For instance, you can see this sometimes in the way men and women make their needs known. Men tend to be more forthright and aggressive about what they want. Women tend to test the community's disposition about a felt need first, and then they may or may not act on their own desire. This can be noted whether the need is a class scheduling conflict, a roommate's cleaning responsibility or just being thirsty.

Take Harry and Sally, for example. They are walking down the street together. Harry is thirsty and passes a drugstore. He says to Sally, "I want a Coke. I'll just pop in here and get one.

You want one too?" Harry is thirsty. Harry decides what he wants and independently plans to fulfill his desire.

Okay. Same scene. But now Sally is thirsty. She asks Harry, "Are you thirsty?" Depending on his answer and the degree of her thirst, she may or may not actually stop in the store and buy something to drink. If he says no, then she may tend to weigh this lack of interest into her behavior. She may just put off her thirst and keep walking. If he says yes, then her reply may be, "Well, do you want to stop in here and get a Coke?" For Sally, what to do about her need tends to be a decision to be made together as a "community."

Now there is no better or worse way in all of this. Harry is not better because he is more straightforward and decisive. Sally is not better because she wants to know if Harry is thirsty too. Harry is not worse because he doesn't initially include Sally in his plans to interrupt their walk. Sally is not worse because she is not as forthright and wants to make a decision together. These friends are, in this scenario, simply tending to be male-ish and female-ish.

This is not to say that men cannot be community-minded and "sensitive" or that women can't be decisive and independent. I have illustrated a tendency within male and female sexuality. Generally, and certainly not without many exceptions, males have to be more intentional in considering community, and females have to be more intentional in manifesting independent decision-making. If male and female tendencies were the same, the experience of living together would be less balanced and a lot less satisfying.

Planet Earth

Despite the popular notion and book, men aren't really from Mars and women aren't really from Venus. We are all from planet Earth, and we can be good friends. We can be better friends if we accept and understand (as much as this is possible) the maleness and femaleness of our sexuality that does make us different from one another.

Gender differences must be respected and honored in a friendship. It can actually wound a woman deeply to be treated like one of the guys. "I want to be a friend, but it bothers me when he talks about other women's feelings as though I don't have the same feelings!" is a complaint I've heard from single women through the years. Similarly, I've had more than a few young men comment about the frustration of being "invisible" as a guy-with-feelings when female friends talk about other guys without regard for who they are as male.

Within a male–female friendship there should be the opportunity to discuss how gender makes a difference in how people think, feel, function and assess the world around them. A man and woman need to ask each other honest questions about a viewpoint that may be wise to consider or feelings that the other may not naturally share. The personal safety and physical vulnerability of women needs to be a concern to men. Men need to ask, "Would you feel safe?" in certain situations. Women tend to be more accurately intuitive in assessing group dynamics and the unspoken rules of a social or professional situation. Men may find it helpful to ask a woman what she thinks or even feels about a new situation or the interpersonal relationships that may be important for understanding others.

The inclination for men to be more private and less verbal needs to be respected by women. We need to give men time to *think* about what they *feel*. This extra step on the way to understanding feelings is less needed in women. We women can often talk about how we feel and just feel what we feel; understanding comes from the dialogue. Women need to accept that men have a tendency not to verbalize what they feel until they have had the time to think about what they feel and, often, why they feel the way they do.

Probably the most comfortable male–female friendship can

take place between siblings. Brothers and sisters, especially if they are close in age, can be a great help or a great aggravation.

What we learn about the opposite sex by living with a brother or sister can be enhanced by actually talking to them! If you have a brother or sister, ask them about how they feel or think about specific situations as a male or female. Listen to each other. Don't pass judgment on the assessment or feeling; just listen and consider. We may not understand why a person thinks or feels the way they do, but we can note the tendency and accept what we hear.

The Family of God
Brothers and sisters in the body of Christ should be able to offer the same kind of thoughtful acceptance to each other. Friendships that are defined by a common commitment to Christ should offer a trustworthiness and honesty that can be helpful in understanding each other as male and female. We need to ask each other honest questions with no hidden agenda behind what we say. Brothers and sisters in the church should offer each other a safe place to be who we are, ask what we will and grow as women and men of God together. Men and women in the church can learn a lot from each other by listening well in personal conversations, on church committees and in the work of the kingdom.

Equal respect for men and women in the job market, classroom and social circles should not create an androgynous single sex, neither male nor female. Equal opportunity does not eliminate gender-based differences and distinctions. Genesis describes God's intention when the Scripture records, "Male and female he created them" (Genesis 1:27). Sexual distinction was God's idea, not just for marriage and procreation but for all relationships that reflect his image. Paul's summary in Galatians that in Christ there is neither "male nor female" was intended to highlight the inclusiveness of the church family, not negate sexual distinction (Galatians 3:28). We need each other as male and female to be fully human, fully Christian, fully the church and fully able to reflect the image of God.

Common Cause

Male and female together in relationship and work within the family of God honor God's intentions for the human creation. The exclusive union indicated in "be fruitful and increase in number" is one intention. Benevolent dominion over the rest of the created order is the other. When God called the man and woman to work together for the good of God's creation, males and females were commissioned to a relationship focused on a task they can only do together. This is benevolent dominion, an obedience to the instruction of the Creator given before the Fall and given again, with a warning of difficulty, after the Fall.

Common cause and purpose, as well as common values and means, are basics for healthy male–female friendships. Too many friendships today begin and end on the touchy-feely premise that functions only on the energy of the relationship itself. In between the beginning and the end, an unhealthy codependency can exist which excludes any purpose or value greater than the friendship itself. This is eventually dissatisfying, not only to the friends but to God, who has a greater purpose for his creatures and children.

Friendships need a focus greater than those who are involved in the relationship. Events that draw people together around a common cause can often create the atmosphere and opportunity for lifelong friendships, same sex or not. It is important for a friendship not to lose an external focus (work, project, cause, hobby, idea, etc.), even though the focus can change with time.

When two friends ask me for help in a time of relational crisis or difficulty, I often find that the relationship has gotten centered on itself to the exclusion of a common and external interest. Friends who enjoyed working at the homeless shelter or with the church youth group no longer do those things, and they find themselves bored and dissatisfied. Thus feelings are fragile, and the friendship is in peril.

There is certainly wisdom in the caution that relationships, platonic or romantic, find time to just "be" and not always "do," but imbalance is wrong either way. A friendship is a relationship of being *and* doing. What we do together with common values and purpose helps define the edges of who we are in the relationship. Who we are in the relationship fosters the commonality of purpose and values held in the friendship that, together, serves God's greater intention for his creation. Too many friendships fail from becoming ingrown and selfish.

Too many marriages fail for the same reason. In a male-female friendship nurtured and sustained by common purposes and values, we can begin to learn much of what makes a good lifelong married relationship. To satisfy for a lifetime, both friendships and marriages need a focus, a purpose, greater than themselves.

Speaking the Truth in Love

All friendships need to be honest, open and accountable. When the friendship is between a woman and a man, special attention needs to given to this need. The potential for romance, as well as differences in gender-influenced tendencies, can create a subtext to the relationship. Among many possibilities, the subtext may be sexual tension, sexual interest or sexual information. One person may begin to feel differently about the other in a sexual way (sexual interest). This interest may be unexpressed, creating sexual tension, or may be expressed in a less than straightforward way to gain information from the other person about how they may feel. If the other person is unaware of a change in the relationship, misunderstanding can result.

"Speaking the truth in love" is a scriptural mandate for relationships in the body of Christ. We need to tell each other the truth and trust God to give us all the grace we need no matter how the other person responds.

I remember the day I had to "speak the truth in love" to Breck about my feelings in our dating relationship. I felt I was in love with this man, and he needed to know it. I did not think he was at the same point, but my feelings were becoming so intense that not to tell him would have increased the possibility of misunderstanding between us. I could have taken a simple gesture too seriously. He could have taken too lightly something I said or did that had greater meaning for me. I had to be honest.

I was scared. I knew theologically that I could trust God with this relationship. I was convinced that God wanted "the best" for me. I just wanted *Breck* to be "the best." To really trust God meant I had to trust that God could honor honesty in the relationship. I had to tell Breck what I felt.

"Speaking the truth in love" when I was in love felt really risky that day. It was a gorgeous, sunny day. We sat on a park bench watching the pigeons in Jackson Square in the middle of the New Orleans French Quarter. In the course of the conversation I told Breck I had to tell him something. As I recall, I said something like "I believe that I have fallen in love with you. I am having a hard time imagining my life apart from you. I don't think you quite share this feeling now, but you need to know where I'm at. You need to be careful with my feelings in this relationship."

I don't remember all of our conversation, but Breck did say he appreciated knowing how I felt and that I was correct in guessing that he was not where I was emotionally. He said he would be careful with my feelings and would try not to do or say anything that would not clearly reflect his real level of commitment to the relationship. I do remember that he said,

"Robbie, I promise never to say the words 'I love you' unless I mean them for a lifetime."

I was so relieved. He had listened. He wasn't afraid of my feelings. He hadn't run away! And he had promised a mutual honesty in the relationship. All of a sudden I was relaxed again. The truth had been spoken in love and heard with grace. We could be friends honestly and continue to explore the relationship with integrity and care.

Not too long after that day in the park, we were driving up I-59 on the way to a picnic. Breck said with humorous nonchalance, "Oh, yeah, I've been meaning to tell you something. I love you. And it's forever." He looked over at me with a big smile. We had a great picnic.

Attraction and Distraction

Knowing where you are in a friendship like this is important. Being honest with your own feelings and caring for the feelings of the other person can be of immeasurable value. In a long-term friendship, it may be wise to take it less for granted and think about the relationship and what it means for each of you from time to time.

Recently I was with an unmarried friend in his late twenties. We talked about relationships, and a particular long-lasting friendship he had with a young woman who lived back home. He admitted that he didn't think he "loved" her. His reason, he revealed with some hesitation, was that she didn't "look like" the person he always thought he would marry. He just knew he thought about her every day and found several things within a day's experience that he wanted to tell her about. He missed their friendship more than he'd thought he would when he left for graduate school. He talked about her with enthusiasm, commenting on their common goals and values. He respects her work and contribution to community and church. She understands his goals and values, many of which she shares.

There was obviously a comfortable compatibility between them. They had a valuable friendship that might or might not become a married relationship.

I think I was able to help my friend value this friendship more highly. He needed to see that the interests that they held in common, their past history of shared experiences and mutually held values, were more significant than he supposed for evaluating the relationship. He also began to consider that Hollywood might have had more to do with what he imagined love to be than he wanted to admit. I reassured him this was pretty common and told him about the time I discovered Breck had the same misgivings about me.

We had become officially engaged and were attending a youth conference with a group from Breck's church. Intending to borrow a sheet of paper from a notebook Breck had with him, I came across this prayer he had written before our engagement:

Dear God,

How do I know if I am in love? In what can I find certainty?

Something bothers me. She's not as pretty as I had always anticipated my wife being. And she's not as shapely as I have always wanted my wife to be. Does that really matter? I want to say no, but still I am made uneasy by this gap.

Something good is there too. I respect her confidence and enthusiasm about who she is and who you are. I have learned from her to love more the life you give us. She is vibrant and happy, and she wants to do nice things for me and she has.

I can't forget her. We seem to have a natural intimacy. I think I love her, Lord.

Your son,

Breck

Now, it was a little unsettling to read those words just a few months before we intended to say "I do"! I looked at Breck as we sat side by side in this huge auditorium, and he blushed as he realized what I had just read. He leaned closer, put his arm around me and whispered in my ear, "Oh, that was a lifetime ago. You are more beautiful to me than you can ever imagine."

I believed him—not just because of the love in his eyes and the tenderness in his voice, but because of the conduct rules we'd had to set to keep our hands in the realm of holiness. Something about me sure seemed attractive enough!

Little did Breck know in the early days, as love carved a niche in his heart, that I would become so beautiful to him and so dear. In the early days of our friendship, little did I know that Breck would be the only man that I would ever love. The "Grand Canyon" of our marriage began with the insistent trickle of a natural intimacy, an intimation that our friendship carried a special intention and would develop into a lifelong romance. This happened as we appreciated each other and noted each other's gifts and talents and attributes. It happened as we began to share work and ministry together. We discovered common goals and values. The means we used to ends were compatible and comfortable.

Romance also blossomed from our friendship as we both let go of Hollywood's ideas of what makes a person beautiful or handsome. We faced disappointments and confessed the same to the Lord. Neither of us was perfect for the other. How can two imperfect people, admitted sinners theologically and practically, ever be perfect for each other? What we both discovered in our friendship was that we were, in an unusual way, good for each other. We were better people together than apart. We were more faithful as pilgrims on the journey when we shared the road together.

We fell in love in 1971. And today if you were to stand near the rim of our lives, you would see something deep and wide and beautiful.

5

Emotional Fornication
& Other No-Nos

SPEAKING THE TRUTH in love grows out of the freedom felt in a secure relationship. Friends who really trust each other can speak the truth in love. Two friends who are being honest with each other, as well as kind to one another, are free to explore the possibilities of how their relationship develops as they edge toward Eden. When truthfulness and kindness are not intentionally and explicitly part of a dating relationship, it may be because the development of a trusting friendship has not occurred.

Good friendships can be established fairly quickly or very slowly. Truth, not time, is the key factor in a relationship or friendship that honors God. Unfortunate emotional entanglements often happen when dating begins before a friendship is established.

Unless a mutually similar commitment is identified and openly shared in a relationship, emotional fornication can result. Premarital sex isn't the only way to "get ahead of yourself" in a relationship. A romantic relationship can create an emotional tangle between people that they can't untie. Two people don't quite know how they got where they are with each other, feelings are assumed and unidentified, and people get hurt.

A relationship is out of sync when behavior within the relationship does not match the commitments needed to sustain the relationship. Premarital emotional intercourse. Emotional fornication. Lovers become enemies because they were never friends. It happens all the time.

Charlotte and Eddie

The only thing Charlotte and Eddie had in common was their last name. C. Berry and E. Berry were assigned seats next to each other in two classes during their freshman year. They talked after the second class and laughed about the odds of being together in two intro classes of over eighty students in a school of twenty-four thousand with teachers who took attendance by seat assignment! Charlotte invited Eddie to a concert by a Christian recording artist that weekend. Her intention wasn't really to date but to gauge Eddie's reaction to the "Christian" label. Was he a Christian or wasn't he? She'd been cautioned by her youth-group leader to date only Christians. This had never been a big problem to Charlotte. She'd only had a few dates in high school, but she'd gone off to college hoping to date more. She certainly intended to try to date only a Christian when it got serious. As a freshman, Charlotte just wanted to date, and it would be all the better if he was a Christian.

Eddie was positive about the invitation, recognized the name of the performer and mentioned a few things about a church back home. Charlotte was nice-looking and friendly, and he wanted to meet people. They walked as far as they could together until they had to split for different buildings. Before they parted, Eddie asked Charlotte to meet him at a restaurant near campus for dinner that night. Charlotte was surprised but pleased and said okay. This was a Tuesday.

The dinner was pleasant, tasty and full of small talk. They made plans to meet between classes the next day, to study together for the Thursday classes they had in common and to go out again Friday night. Tuesday evening ended with a brief hug and an awkward brush against each other's cheek.

Wednesday's greeting included a longer hug, and Wednesday night's study session ended with a kiss that lingered. Thursday's classes were tense and distracting. They needed to talk that night. Charlotte suggested they meet at the stadium; it was open for students who would run the steps, and the bleachers provided a great place to talk. They met. They talked a little and ended up kissing a lot. Charlotte and Eddie both felt they had found each other in a sea of people and this Friday night would not be dateless and boring. They felt good about each other, and they felt good about themselves.

Charlotte's friends in the campus fellowship were more than a little surprised when she came to the concert on Saturday holding hands with Eddie. Her closer friends had heard about the interest, but the relationship looked a lot further along than only five days would indicate. Eddie was nice and liked Charlotte's friends. He was invited to one of the campus Bible studies organized by the fellowship. He said okay, but Charlotte sensed he was just being polite and wasn't really interested. Her first thought was to quit her women's study and move to a coed study that Eddie might like to attend. She intended to talk to him about it later.

In the next few weeks, the joy of being hugged and kissed and belonging to someone was deeply satisfying. Charlotte and Eddie liked each other. During their more intimate times they even said they loved each other. Both were sexually inexperienced, so intercourse was not a part of their relationship. Besides that, Charlotte had always wanted to wait until marriage because she was a Christian.

This hesitation bothered Eddie some, but he really liked

Charlotte and would try to understand. She seemed a bit too religious for him, but he had always wanted something a little deeper in his life. Maybe this was it. He was a little uneasy when Charlotte joked about not having to change her last name or get a new driver's license if they got hitched. But he laughed and said they could hyphenate their names and be the "Berry-Berrys" *if* anything did happen.

Unspoken and concealed uneasiness between them increased. Charlotte began to think Eddie was a little spiritually lazy. He always found a good excuse not to attend Bible study or church. Eddie began to think that Charlotte was a little too controlling. He felt they always ended up following her agenda. Charlotte wished Eddie would shave more often. Eddie wished Charlotte would show off her figure a little more. Charlotte wondered why Eddie never talked about his family. Eddie wondered why Charlotte talked to her mother every day. They wondered, and they wished. And they kissed and hugged and spent weekend evenings together. They held hands and made plans to spend a lot of fall break together at Charlotte's home.

Charlotte skipped the fellowship retreat because Eddie had to work and couldn't go. Eddie wanted to play on his dorm's intramural team but didn't because Charlotte wasn't all that interested. Each began to question what it was that they found interesting in the other. Besides being an "item," there was little on the list. Both thought it might be the time to push the relationship a little further over fall break. Each wanted to feel more genuine in the relationship.

During fall break, sexual boundaries were crossed just short of intercourse. Most of it felt really good. It had to be right, they told each other, because they did love each other. It was getting more difficult to spend lots of time with each other without physically going "too far." Both were relieved when break was over and school would put some structure around their time. Four days together suddenly seemed like an awfully long time.

Charlotte and Eddie said "I love you" many times, but both wondered what the other meant by that.

Back on campus, Eddie decided to join the intramural team, and Charlotte began to wonder why being with Eddie didn't feel like it used to feel. She found herself trying to be more sexually accommodating to restore the original thrill. At the same time Eddie seemed less interested and more distant than ever. There was a routine in the relationship that displayed all the assumptions of being permanent. They did what was expected and what had always been a part of their relationship. Charlotte and Eddie had each other. What they didn't have was a friendship.

They didn't make plans for the longer Christmas break, and neither of them talked about why they didn't. They gave each other gifts. Sweaters. They had a lingering and passionate goodby for the holidays, but each discovered a sense of relief in being apart. Phone calls were exchanged over Christmas, but there wasn't much to talk about.

Eddie finally brought up the idea that they date other people. Charlotte cried and wondered what happened to love. She was glad she hadn't gone "all the way" with Eddie, but she wondered if it would have helped them stay together if she had been more willing. Both of them missed a steady date and an outlet for some sexual tension. But neither ever really missed a friend.

This is a picture, drawn from several true stories, of emotional fornication. Charlotte and Eddie began a dating relationship without establishing a friendship. They got tangled up in each other's lives and met their own emotional needs through what the other would give. Both moved away from their own identities to be an "item." Both gave up friendships and activities of personal interest to keep a hold on the relationship. Charlotte neglected her faith while Eddie redefined his. They said the word *love* to each other, but they didn't talk to each other.

The social and physical comforts of the relationship seemed worth the price of all other losses for a while. Then they just lost interest and didn't want to admit it. The emotional intercourse of their lives continued until Eddie pulled away.

The damaging effects of this relationship didn't end with the breakup. Eddie made up his mind not to date any more "religious" girls. He was a good guy, he told himself, and deserved more in a relationship. The next girl he dated had no problem with sex as long as it was safe. It was fun. Eddie established a pattern of dating, having fun and being a nice guy when he broke up. He just hasn't established any friendships along the way. Eddie is still alone.

Charlotte was lonely. She really missed physical affection and the fun of dating and going out places. She got more involved with the campus fellowship but didn't get any dates. She also didn't develop any good friendships with women in the group. They saw her as a chronic flirt. She was always coming on to the guys in the group and almost always preferred male conversation and company. The men in the fellowship thought she tried too hard and flirted with every guy there. No one felt like they knew the real Charlotte. She just played around being whoever she thought others wanted her to be.

Charlotte wasn't looking for a friend, just a date. And she didn't get what she wanted in the fellowship. So she dated the first guy who asked her out. They met in a calculus study group during her sophomore year. Charlotte didn't want to lose this guy when he pressed for more sexually as they continued to date. She got pregnant. He transferred to another school closer to his home. Charlotte finished school at the price of a painful secret that she hasn't shared with anyone. Not her mom. Not God. And not a friend. Charlotte doesn't feel close to anyone and doesn't want to. A friend might get too close and find out who she really is. Charlotte is still alone.

Emotional Fornication

Emotional fornication is damaging. This emotional entanglement without commitment takes two people in an unexamined direction toward an intimacy that is emotionally beyond any sense of commitment they are ready to make to each other. Emotional fornication is relationally manipulative. It uses the other person for its own satisfaction. It feeds off the relationship and does not establish or enhance a friendship. Emotional fornication happens anytime a part of a relationship gets out of sync with the reality of commitment that each person *explicitly* brings to it.

Emotional fornication does not speak the truth in love. It is not love, and it has not talked about what is true. It just happens. Unexamined. Not talked about. It is a tangled web of feelings between two people who have no idea how to tie a knot that will hold the weight of the relationship. Emotional fornication can make enemies out of people who were never friends.

It can also end a friendship. This can happen when there is a change from a friendship to a dating relationship and the process has been left unexamined and undefined. Friends with common values and goals may share a task or responsibility. They spend a lot of time together. They do get to know each other. They share confidences, as friends do. They give each other advice and listen to each other well.

Unlike the premise promoted in the movie *When Harry Met Sally*, it *is* possible for men and women to have a friendship without a romantic relationship. Honesty with yourself as well as the other person is the guardian of the friendship.

Saying what is meant and meaning what is said prevents a lot of misunderstanding, frustration and heartbreak. Speaking the truth in love preserves a lot of friendships, leads to many marriages and satisfies more than a few hearts. Examining and expressing what a person thinks or feels about another is important. Friendships are dynamic. They change as the friends involved change. A healthy friendship that serves and satisfies both people is necessarily an honest friendship.

Martin and Julia

Martin and Julia were both committed Christians. Martin was in his first year of teaching elementary school, and Julia was an insurance claims examiner. They went to the same church, and both volunteered with the high-school youth group. Martin was also employed by the church as the pianist and leader of the worship team. Julia sang in the choir and had been a member since her college days. They held common faith and common values and spent a lot of time together involved in the work of the church.

They went a lot of places together, usually with the youth group or with other friends in the church. They got together frequently to plan youth retreats and weekly meetings. They were comfortable in each other's company and accepted invitations together to attend various functions. They sat together to teach the high-school youth and ended up sitting together at the Wednesday-evening Bible study. After several months it seemed natural to see a movie together and to cook for each other on occasion.

Walking into a movie one evening, Julia began to hold Martin's arm. Although Martin was surprised by this expression of affection, it seemed expected and natural, and he liked it. When they were out alone, he began to hold her hand, kiss her goodnight and wonder if this was "the one" for him.

Julia began to assume that Martin was "the one" for her. It seemed to be what everyone expected. Somewhere along the line both Martin and Julia began to use "we" as the language of referring to each other. Both had said "I love you" on the right occasions. They kissed and caressed a little, but both were careful not to let their physical relationship go "too far."

Two years later Martin and Julia were still the expected sweethearts of the church, the envy of the high-schoolers and the hope of their parents for grandchildren "someday."

Julia longed for Martin to "pop the question" and give the relationship some definite direction. Martin never thought about it. Everyone assumed they would marry, and they probably would, but Martin felt things were okay for now the way they were. Neither Julia or Martin ever talked about where they were in the relationship. They never talked about how the relationship had evolved in the first place. Julia wasn't honest with Martin about her need for some security. Martin wasn't honest with himself about Julia's habits that he found annoying.

Eventually Martin began to sense that Julia's commitment to the relationship was more intense than his. He wasn't sure what he wanted, but he was willing to go along to see how the relationship developed. But it didn't develop. From Julia's point of view, she and Martin were at a standstill. She was frustrated, increasingly resentful and unconsciously (because she wasn't honest with herself or Martin about her feelings) pushed her expectations of what a couple-in-love was supposed to look like. Julia kept track of Martin's schedule, cooked for him several times a week and wanted to do his laundry, but he wouldn't let her.

This constant pursuit of emotional intimacy bothered Martin, but he didn't know why. He found himself creating excuses not to eat with Julia. He began to make excuses to not do things as much together. He felt himself leaving the relationship as he had entered the relationship. It just began to happen.

One night when Martin again excused himself from being with her, Julia finally asked an honest question. "You are breaking up with me, aren't you?" Martin denied it at the time, but her question forced him to be honest about what he did feel about the relationship and about Julia. Martin concluded honestly that he didn't really love her. For some reason he couldn't say, he knew he did not want to spend the rest of his life with this person. He had been a user in the relationship, and he knew it. He had been comfortable with it for some time, but had known that Julia wanted more. He had to admit that he never had wanted more in the relationship, but had been willing to create his own comfort zone for nearly two and a half years.

A week later, when the breakup was official, it was really painful. Martin felt like the louse he had been. He had been selfish and unfair, and this is hard to admit when you've thought you were doing your best. Julia was angry and hurt. She felt personal failure and deep rejection. She was in love, and her heart was broken.

Martin had no idea what Julia felt. Julia had no idea what Martin thought. Not from the beginning. And not at the end.

Unexamined expectations and assumptions ended what had been a good friendship. Emotional fornication, urged by Julia and accepted by Martin, had blinded them to their own feelings and made it nearly impossible to be honest with each other. They had been on a "blind" date for two and a half years and never knew it.

Julia finally felt she had to attend another church. It was just too painful to see Martin week after week, and he was employed by the church and was less likely to leave.

Martin and Julia survived. They learned a painful lesson about speaking the truth in love and continued to grow as disciples in the Christian faith. They each married a fellow believer and eventually had children. In separate towns and lives they have both told their story of each other. They have regrets about who they were, how they acted and why it had to hurt so badly. Martin and Julia have learned some lessons and gained some wisdom. They each married as physical virgins, but emotional fornication left its scar on each of their hearts.

Virginity Redefined

The penetration of emotional will before a convenantal commitment can destroy lives. *Virginity* is commonly a technical term that needs some redefinition. People can give themselves away emotionally without genital intercourse. Men and women "give their hearts" to each other without a mutual commitment to each other. Keeping the verbal, physical, social, religious, mental and emotional expressions within a relationship in tune and in time with the commitment level of a relationship is healthy. The possibility of emotional fornication can actually increase when physical sexual expressions are held in check and intimacy beyond commitment is sought in other areas of the relationship.

Premarital sex causes emotional scars even if the relationship results in marriage. People don't forget sexual encounters in their souls or deepest memories. Scripture makes it clear that "becoming one" takes place when two bodies are united. There is more than the physical dynamic that impacts that sexual act. Genitals don't have sex. People do. Whole people. Body-and-soul people. Issues of fidelity and holiness matter in physical activities of sexuality.

Self-control, as a fruit of the Spirit, can be exercised in more areas than physical intercourse. It is appropriate and obedient to the mandate of Scripture to "guard your heart" (Proverbs 4:23). Exercising honesty in every area of a relationship is a good way to continue a friendship. Speaking the truth in love is a wise way to guard your heart. Time, talk and touch are three of the areas in a relationship that can be used to understand and evaluate what is really going on between friends who want to explore the possibilities of lifelong love as they journey toward Eden.

6

Let's Talk

IF FRIENDSHIPS ARE to be the bedrock of eventual married relationships, the idea of dating before friendship should be examined. There can be a lot of unwanted and unnecessary baggage with dating as a prelude to acquaintance with another person. Allowing a special interest in a person to grow from a natural friendship can minimize miscommunication and misconstrued expectations. It is much easier to relax and really be yourself in the beginnings of a dating relationship if the person you date is already a friend. The often painful emotional entanglements caused by dating without friendship can be avoided if you adopt a different social pattern in getting to know the opposite sex.

It is wise to recognize and admit that there is a difference between going out with "just a friend" and dating someone. This needs to be clearly communicated if the relationship changes. Often a group of friends will go places and do things together for a time, and out of those friendships a special interest in another person will emerge.

A dating relationship begins when the romantic potential of the friendship is acknowledged openly. Yes, this acknowledgment is possible and necessary. A clear indication or declaration of intention or interest is a mark of maturity. This is an essential exercise in speaking the truth in love. Christians too often uncritically embrace the game-playing patterns inherent in the North American dating tradition. Flirtatious hinting is oblique in approach and immature.

Carmen and Earl

A young woman came to me for some advice. She needed insight into how to discern the nature of the relationship between her and a young man in the campus fellowship they both attended. I had noticed that Carmen and Earl had come together to several meetings, and I had seen them together and greeted them at a restaurant where my husband and I had dined. When we were together I asked Carmen, "Are you and Earl dating now?" I knew they had been good friends for some time and had led a campus Bible study together. I thought they might just make a good couple. Carmen replied, "Well, I don't know. That's what I want to talk to you about."

Carmen told me that they were seeing "more and more" of each other just one on one, but there had been no romantic expression within the relationship from either of them. Carmen admitted to me that she would be open to this but wanted Earl to initiate this transition. "I wouldn't mind if he took my hand, or put his arm around me, or just let me know if we are actually 'dating,' " Carmen confessed. She made it clear, when I asked, that they had never talked about their friendship. Neither had initiated a conversation about whether there had been a change in the expectations of their relationship. Carmen felt, and rightly so, that this needed to happen.

Carmen very clearly expressed the questions she had about her friendship with Earl. "Does he have an interest in me that goes beyond a sister-in-Christ friendship? If we are not 'dating,' why do we spend so much of our free time just with each other? Although we haven't been romantic, I wonder if Earl would be hurt if I did begin to date someone else." Carmen ended by saying, "One problem with my feelings is that I really don't have any desire to date or explore a romantic relationship with anyone else but Earl. I just don't know what he is thinking and don't want to lose a friend if he's not interested in a different kind of relationship."

My basic advice was (and has been on many similar occasions with others), "Carmen, you need to tell your friend what you just told me." This is exactly how you exercise faith and speak the truth in love. You don't bring expectations to how the questions might be answered; you simply ask the questions. You discuss the friendship and objectify the relationship.

Carmen's response was "You're kidding!" I assured her I was not.

Speaking the truth in love is essential in a married relationship. Why don't we practice this pattern in friendships and dating relationships? It can be done. It needs to be done.

A few days later, Carmen and Earl talked about where they were in their friendship. Earl was more than relieved to tell her, "Yes, I'd like to think of us as dating. I haven't held your hand or anything because I didn't know what you'd do. I've thought about it, but I didn't want to crash and burn."

Well, Carmen and Earl didn't "crash and burn." They maturely began to explore the romantic possibilities of their friendship, became engaged about six months later, married within a year and now have three kids. And they still practice speaking the truth in love.

Patrice and Greg

Another young couple had a similar conversation and decided to date for a time, but discovered that their future goals were pretty far apart. Patrice had a tremendous burden for working with alcoholics in an urban setting. Her education and training suited her well for this. Greg was in soil management and was heading for a long-term mission in rural Africa. They came to a time when they discussed the basic incompatibility of their vocational callings and agreed to maintain their friendship and trust the Lord to provide lifelong partners who would better share their lives. Patrice and Greg remained friends and met and married other people. Chicago and Ethiopia are both blessed.

It is not easy or comfortable to speak the truth in love—even for Christians in our culture and time. The discomfort and reticence don't come just from concerns about how to say what is meant, but from the very idea itself. The risk of being known honestly is an issue of faith. The exercise of faith makes us vulnerable. And humble. The outcome of honesty is not guaranteed, but honesty is honored by God. Speaking the truth in love is the basic language of a servant of Jesus Christ. Carmen and Earl, Patrice and Greg needed to be servants of each other as brothers and sisters in Christ.

Carmen desired to be an honest friend to Earl, and to do that she needed to understand his expectations and relate her own interests. Patrice and Greg served one another by placing each other's interests and training above their own desires for a romantic relationship. Honesty isn't above risk, but it is worth the risk. God is good and wants to be good to his children. And he wants his children to be good to each other. Speaking the truth in love is good for us. This idea needs to be less novel—especially within the family of God.

Three Good Questions

We can ask ourselves three good questions while learning how to be honest and good friends to others. These questions are not just advisable for opposite-sex friendships but all relationships.

First, "Is it *true?*" Of course no falsehood is ever wise. Actually, there is one exception given by the ancient rabbis of the Jewish faith: every bride is a beautiful bride. I think there may be one about babies being cute and the dead being good, but I'm not sure! Anyway, the point is that the truth matters. In things of the heart, it is important to understand the truth of what you feel or think as clearly as possible. There may be times when the truth of how you feel is unclear. That lack of clarity will need to be confessed as the truth. "I don't know" can be an honest expression of the truth. Guard against expressions or platitudes that are not true. Don't lie to yourself or the other person about your relationship.

Second, "Is it *necessary?*" Sometimes the truth doesn't need expression. Okay, this newborn baby really might be ugly, but no mother needs to hear you mention that! Okay, the altos in the choir were really flat, but is it necessary that you tell them? Only if you are the choir director. Was it necessary for Carmen to talk to Earl? Yes. She was increasingly uneasy with her own feelings and frustrated by not knowing how Earl felt. It took some counsel and prayer to identify the truth of her feelings, and then it became necessary to share them. But how?

That involves the third question, "Is it *loving?*" Yes, it may be true that the altos were flat. Yes, as the choir director, you need to tune them in to this fact. But how can you inform them of this with love? Well, not in front of the congregation or in the choir loft right after worship. Most true, necessary and loving conversations include only the people involved. And most true, necessary and loving conversations take place when there is actually time to communicate. There needs to be time to hear, not just to say what needs to be said.

Carmen decided to speak the truth in love to her friend Earl after his physics exam and not during the stressful evening when he studied for it. Carmen didn't pull Earl aside as people were arriving for their Bible study to have this talk. She waited until they had one-on-one time, undistracted by others or pressured by time. Timing has a lot to do with what makes something loving. If it's the truth and it's necessary, it is worth the right time.

A wise choir director will ask the choir to evaluate their own efforts. The sopranos may say, "Well, there was something not quite right." The altos may confess, "We were flat!" But any choir not entirely tone-deaf will know it could have been better. The choir wants to be good. Out of that desire, the director works with the altos to make them better.

People generally want good relationships. We want good friendships. That desire needs to create a pattern in our lives to be truthful, careful and loving. Is it true? Is it necessary? Is it loving? These three questions make us better servants, friends and spouses.

Loving Honestly

As advisable as these questions are, the results aren't always what we hoped for. An alto might feel maligned and quit the choir. Earl could have responded out of some basic insecurity he harbored and never have asked Carmen to dinner again. Patrice and Greg might have been so lonely that one or the other would sacrifice a personal calling and live forever after with a nagging sense of regret. Immaturity *can be* a response to mature, necessary and loving honesty. Immaturity is *guaranteed* for anything other than that.

Speaking the necessary truth in love makes for better friends and better choirs. It also makes for a better romance. "Relaxing romance" is not an oxymoron when all that is said and done is true, necessary and loving. The stress experienced when friendships make the transition to an exploration of romantic possibilities can be transformed through honest talk about the relationship. The satisfaction of a healthy friendship can be enhanced when both friends know that there is no other agenda behind the scenes. Friends can be supportive of each other as relationships change.

We Is a Big Word

Talk within a romance needs the same kind of thoughtful care and can be a dependable barometer to help assess the relationship. The use of the first-person plural pronoun, the two-letter word *we,* can indicate volumes about what a person thinks about a relationship. "*We* went there. *We* called them. *We* bought this." When "we" becomes part of a dating vocabulary, it signals a change from a casual to a serious relationship. In a healthy relationship, when two people are emotionally synchronized and equally committed to each other, becoming a "we" in conversation happens at about the same time. "We" without this mutual timing and commitment can be an early signal of emotional fornication and unhealthy imbalance in the relationship.

I have been in more than a few conversations when *we* was used as the pronoun of choice, without an initial indication of who the other person was who made up the "we." Assumptions were being made, not only about my knowledge of the relationship but also about the relationship itself. "We went to Orlando to see my folks over spring break." When I asked who was "we," the response was something like "Oh, you know, Ron and I" (or "Rhonda and I"). In such a conversation I might go on to comment that the relationship must be "pretty serious." If the gap was just my lack of information and the relationship is well on its way to a lifelong commitment, then fine. However, if *we* is used casually to undergird important *hopes* for the relationship, caution may be in order.

Are both people thinking of each other in "we" terms, or is it just one person? What does each person feel, anticipate and think about the future of the relationship? Have the two people making up this "we" talked about where they are in the relationship? Is one person feeling pressured into some sort of commitment or future they are not clear about or ready for?

The language used within a relationship can help monitor and assess where each person is in the development of the relationship. *We* is a short word that usually needs to be kept in use for a long-term relationship. Self-reference is an important key to hearing ourselves say what we think about who we are. When *I* becomes *we,* this is significant. It signals a change in personal freedom, autonomy and selfhood. This can be good or bad depending on whether there is a mutual sense of commitment of the *I*'s involved in the *we.*

The Language of Love

Terms of endearment are less subtle indicators of the same dynamic. Usually people are more intentional and careful when "sweetheart," "dear," "honey" or some other increasingly intimate address is used for the other person. The inclusion of these terms is often a social signal to others of an increasingly exclusive relationship. Care needs to be given when this language emerges in a relationship. Diminutive terms ("sweetie," "my little honey") often signal a special care for something or someone seen as precious or rare. Terms of endearment need to be used with a serious regard for one's own heart as well as the heart of the one addressed.

What two people talk about can also be used to help evaluate a friendship, a romantic relationship or a time of transition between the two. There is a big difference between "What do you like on your bagels?" and "What size boxers do you wear?" Being conscious of the level of intimacy within a conversation is wise. It is a smart way to guard your heart. Being honest about what is comfortable to talk about in a relationship or not is part of defining where a person is in a relationship. True confessions of all past sins on a first Coke–and–movie date may not be wise. Not discussing the issue of birth control before one's wedding is equally unwise.

The depth of what is shared about one's family life or personal history needs to be thoughtfully considered. There is a time and a place for revealing and discussing the deeper issues of our lives. I have been asked by both young men and women beginning a romantic relationship for advice about "when" or "if" to tell the other person about past intimacies. Some of these inquires have been clearly premature. All he did was ask her out for dinner, and before the entree she tells him about her "high-school mistake." The confession exposed an assumption about the future of this dating relationship that may have been the furthest thing from his mind.

If being premature in talking about earlier intimacies is fairly common, so is a prolonged delay in talking about important issues. A couple would be unwise to become engaged without discussing one person's history of exposure to some serious pornography that may affect the increasingly intimate sexual relationship in marriage. What you want to talk about and *don't* want to talk about can tell you a lot about where you are in the relationship. Thinking about the meaning of talk, the language, within a relationship is one barometer to help avoid emotional fornication. Being careful and thoughtful about conversation, language, expressions and terms of endearment can help a couple keep their relationship synchronized emotionally.

St. James writes in his epistle that the tongue is a small part of the body, but like the rudder of a ship, it gives direction to the whole (James 3:2-8). It's a spark that can set a forest on fire. The talk within a relationship can reveal much. What is talked about? What is not talked about? How are things talked about? How do individuals verbally identify the relationship? How is the other person addressed or referred to?

All these things matter. Is it true? Is it necessary? Is it loving? Listening to ourselves and to each other, being careful and fully conscious of the language used in the relationship are important things to consider in assessing a friendship, a romantic relationship or the transition time between the two.

Wise counsel from an independent third party can help assess the communication within a relationship. Learning each other's "love language" is a challenge! What one person does or says to mean "I love you" may not be understood by the one loved. Personal histories color the way a person communicates "I love you."

Edwin and Doris

How money is spent in a relationship can say a lot. An engaged couple came to my husband and me for premarital counseling. In the course of our helping them learn each other's "love language," a difference surfaced in their attitudes about eating out. Doris thought eating out was a big waste of money. Her parents never ate out. Her mother had been a gourmet cook, and her "love language" had been great home-cooked meals. Likewise, Doris said "I love you" by cooking her specialties for Edwin. Edwin, on the other hand, had a wonderful father who treated his mother "like a queen." Edwin's father loved to take Mom out to new restaurants to enjoy new foods, and for Edwin this was a fond memory of how his parents loved each other. Edwin wanted to say "I love you" to Doris in a similar way. Doris and Edwin had two different love languages.

Doris couldn't hear "I love you" in the tradition of eating out that Edwin brought to the relationship. Edwin couldn't hear "I love you" in Doris's insistence that eating at home was the most loving tradition. In the course of counsel, they were able to share these family histories with each other. Doris began to see that eating out wasn't a challenge to her abilities; it was one way Edwin said "I love you." Edwin began to see that Doris's hard work in preparing meals was an expression of affection, not just a way to save money. They began to learn to hear "I love you" in each other's language.

Valentines
I remember learning to hear "I love you" in a new language on Valentine's Day. I am a hopeless romantic. In my home tradition, love and affection were expressed by giving the loved person something they would not buy for themselves—something that was a treat, not necessarily useful. One Valentine's Day I opened a gift from my husband, and I was confused. In the box were towels. Yes, bath towels. Towels were not my idea of love language. Especially for Valentine's Day. I must admit these were nice towels. Thick and heavy.

I tried to be grateful, but Breck knew me too well. That night he handed me a bouquet of flowers (now this was an "I love you" gift that spoke to me!) and said, "I got the feeling that the towels didn't thrill you."

I confessed, "Well, they are just so practical! Nice, and needed, but practical!" I explained that in my love language, romantic gifts should not be practical.

Then Breck explained that in his love language, the best gifts were very practical. At that moment it dawned on me why he always seemed more excited about a tool he needed than by a cute little contribution to his collection of mallard ducks.

That night we agreed to work on thinking of each other's love language in our gift giving. I would be more practical. He would be more "unnecessary." Because we talked about it, I heard "I love you" in those towels. And for his birthday, a few months later, he got some more towels! He was thrilled. This still makes little sense to me. But I am learning to speak his language of love. We are edging a little closer to Eden.

The talk in a relationship, verbal and nonverbal, gives vital information about what is really going on, who is actually involved, where the friendship is headed and why something is important or not. There is no substitute in any relationship for learning each other's love language. Speaking the truth in love and hearing the truth in love are habits of the heart that guard this wellspring of life.

7

Timing
Is Everything

TIME, AS WELL AS TALK, is an able guardian of the heart. How much time is spent and how time is used can be reliable references to use in evaluating a relationship. The transition between a friendship and a potentially romantic relationship is often marked by a change in the amount of time invested in being together. This transition can even be marked by an intensification of the desire to be together when circumstances keep two people apart. Unhealthy tendencies in a relationship can be exposed by how one person thinks about the other's use of time. Emotional fornication can be apparent where an accountability of a person's time is out of proportion to the mutual commitment level present in a relationship.

Alice and Jerry
Alice was more than a little annoyed to hear Jerry's voice on her answering machine ask, "So where are you? You didn't tell me you were going anywhere. Call me when you get back." Alice liked Jerry, and they had been friends for some time be-

fore they began to date each other a month ago. It seemed like a casual relationship to her. Sometimes just the two of them went out, but often they went with a group of friends. For now Alice was comfortable with minimal expressions of affection between them. They held hands, and a good-night kiss was simple, singular and brief.

Jerry liked Alice too. With law school beginning next semester, he was content to take things slowly. He liked having a girlfriend he felt comfortable with, someone he could count on to go places with and talk to. There was so much unsettled in his life, it was nice to have something that was sure and dependable. Jerry had no idea how his assumptions about knowing Alice's whereabouts could undermine their relationship.

Alice felt pressured and crowded by Jerry's message. She had communicated clearly about their mutual time commitments and dates, but she felt he had no reason to need to know her every move. She had never stood him up, was rarely late and had no desire to know everything about his day. He had no business knowing when she went to the grocery store or when she would be back. He had not said he would call about anything. Alice felt this message was demanding and intrusive.

Jerry thought it was an expression of interest in her. Besides, he had just gotten his letter of acceptance from his first choice of law schools, and he wanted to tell her. So where was she? When Jerry phoned again later that night, he was baffled by Alice's general disinterest in his news and hurt that she had not tried to return his call.

This misunderstanding had a degree of innocence in it, but such is not always the case. One member of a relationship can make time accountability an issue that is out of balance with the level of commitment that has been made. The need to know another's schedule can reveal an underlying jealousy. Any sense of "possessing" another person is not a mark of the faith, trust and love needed to build a healthy relationship.

Jerry had no right to know Alice's schedule. He was unwise to leave the message he left, even if he didn't mean it to sound as demanding as it did.

Courtesy, Not Calendars

Friends, platonic or romantic, owe each other courtesy, not calendars. Attitudes about time, together or apart, can tell a lot about a friendship, a romance or a marriage. Part of the wisdom in guarding your heart is trusting each other with matters of time. Evaluating how time is spent, wasted and saved can help avoid the injury and pain that comes from time demands and expectations that are not appropriate to certain seasons of a relationship.

The intensity of Alice's aggravation should prompt her to examine her honest level of contentment in this dating relationship. What does she really feel about Jerry's affection for and interest in her? Is she being honest with herself and with Jerry? She may not be as romantically interested in Jerry as even their modest physical expressions indicate. She needs to make sure she is not misleading him, using his attention or manipulating his time just to have a date.

In the same way, Jerry's eagerness to tell Alice his good news and his disappointment in not knowing where she was should prompt him to examine what he really feels about this woman. How important *is* this relationship to him? What assumptions is he making about Alice's level of romantic interest in him? Is his contentment with the casual nature of their relationship a true reflection of his desire? Can he envision the possibility of a deeper, even lifelong, relationship with Alice? He needs to make sure he is not misleading Alice, using her attention or manipulating her time just to have a date, especially if he honestly desires more than that.

Until two people are mutually committed to a lifelong relationship (engaged or married), any expectation of knowing each other's schedule in detail should be questioned. Of course friends and dating couples will be interested in each other's day-to-day activities, but a desire for a detailed accounting is not appropriate.

Communication of necessary truth with the courtesy inherent in Christlike love is always indicated in any relationship. It is important to remember that "perfect [mature] love drives out fear" (1 John 4:18). Any accounting of time prompted even partially by fear for the relationship is not a good sign.

Resting and Romance

Attitudes about time—time together or time apart—reveal much about a relationship. God's love really does cast out fear, and when we experience godly love there is a level of relaxation within the relationship.

Within the first month of having met Breck, I began to recognize that my relationship with him was distinctively healthy. It felt awfully secure and trustworthy. I was so relaxed in this relationship—could this be "true love"?

The summer we met, my living space in the infirmary did not include a phone, so I received personal calls in the camp director's office. Breck had arranged to call me on a certain weeknight at a certain time. I went to the office to wait for the phone to ring and fell asleep on the couch. The ringing of the phone woke me, and Breck and I had a nice long chat. Toward the end of the conversation Breck apologized for his delay in calling. Until he mentioned it, I hadn't been aware how late it was. He said his meeting went long and he hated to keep me waiting in the office. I told him I had dropped off to sleep and not to worry.

On my walk back through the woods that night, I realized that this was the first time in my life that I had fallen asleep waiting for a guy to call when he said he would. And it wasn't because I was tired. It was because I was relaxed. There was something categorically different about this relationship. It lacked an element of fear. I asked myself, *Is this a hallmark of true love?*

Usually I would have been a nervous wreck. *Will he call? Will he even remember? What will he say? What will we talk about? What does he want? Will we make date plans?* General anxiety had marked even the most casual relationships prior to my romance with Breck. Some of this immaturity came from unfortunate patterns learned from the expectations of the dating-to-get-acquainted routine before I became a Christian. It had taken awhile to unlearn habits of the world when I became a citizen of God's kingdom. Speaking the truth in love is pretty alien outside the family of Father God.

Resting in a relationship and trusting its course to a perfect sovereign Parent is possible only for brothers and sisters in Christ. That summer night I began to wonder if my relationship with Breck could become "the real thing." I stopped briefly and prayed for the Lord to guard my heart, make me wise, continue this sense of trust and help Breck and me keep our eyes on Jesus. The Lord alone is the "author and perfecter of our faith" (Hebrews 12:2) and knows what is going on.

This post–phone call epiphany under the pine trees was underscored by more Scripture. If this was the "peace that surpasses all understanding" that comes from being "anxious for nothing," then I would continue to pray, giving thanks to God. I could trust the Father to be true to his promise. He would "guard my heart and mind through Christ Jesus," and his "peace" would be my gift (see Philippians 4:6–9 NRSV).

Perfect Love Casts Out Fear

This sense of trust wasn't just good for our long-distance dating life, but for our lifetime together. Breck and I spend a lot of time with other people. We spend a fair amount of time away from each other. And we trust each other. This trust is not just grown in the soil of our fallible love, but in the perfect love of God that casts out fear. We pray for each other. We ask that our love be protected and kept only for each other. The failure of so many marriages, within the church as well as without, is sobering. The infidelity and divorce of pastors is heartbreaking. Our lack of fear is the result of our recognition that God must guard our hearts. The price of peace is prayer—prayer to be protected from all the wiles of the evil one, the prowling lion that seeks to devour all who want to honor God (1 Peter 5:8).

I have gone into some detail about this because many people assume too much from the power of their affection for each other. Marriages are not sustained over time by personal affection, but by prayer-guarded fidelity. Faithfulness is a fruit of the Spirit, not good intentions, hormonal needs or keeping track of each other. Courtesy, not calendars, stokes the fires of affection. Courtesy is a part of kindness, another fruit of the Spirit.

The attitude about time in a relationship says a lot about the level of trust between two people. Trust is a measure of maturity as well as security. Maturity in a relationship is marked by courtesy and kindness. And courtesy and kindness need to be elements of how time is used and evaluated in a friendship or romantic relationship.

Time Is a Gift, Not a Threat

How time is spent with each other is important. There is a difference between seeing each other every night and dating just on the weekends. There is a difference between a quick goodby hug and cheek buzz and a good-night that takes the better part of an hour. There is a difference between a whole-day picnic and going for a Coke after a small-group Bible study. There is a difference between planning a vacation around each other's schedule and exchanging addresses so you can write. There is a difference between wanting to do everything with each other—from grocery shopping to church attendance to sharing meals—and making time for a date when each can fit it in.

It is important to be "on the same page" with another person in the investment of time within a relationship. If one person persistently wants more of a person's time than the other desires, resentment and hostility can result. Staying in sync about time use can preserve friendships in the development of a romance. Clear communication about time limits and time expectations can prevent the pain of emotional fornication.

In a good relationship, time is viewed as a generous gift to be well used, not a limited commodity to be manipulated. Spending time together should be invigorating, not exhausting. In fact, one mark of "true love" is that it is generally energizing and contributes to creativity and excellence.

Distracted, but Not Consumed

Love, especially in its early stages, can be distracting. It's a whole new experience. I just visited with a thirtysomething friend who is in love for the first time. He was so pleased to tell me that he and his friend were engaged! It was wonderful to hear what he found delightful in her, how he couldn't wait to see her again and how excited he felt over being loved.

He was delightfully distracted by this romance, but he was not consumed by it. He was not preoccupied to the point that his work suffered, his commitments went unmet or his relationships with others were neglected. Instead, his work was well-focused and well-done. His future plans were sharpened by having someone to share them with. And he expressed to me a distinctive sense of relaxation and depth in his relationships with other people.

I think this feeling of freedom is commonly experienced because engagement and marriage bring a set definition to your other friendships. Many find it less complicated when a friend of the opposite sex is married—intentions are less easily misunderstood. And even same-sex friendships often lose the competitive attitude that can exist ever so subtly between single people.

People in love long for each other's company and look forward to being together. However, this desire lacks jealousy or a need to control the other person. There is a freedom in a love that's real. People become fuller expressions of themselves as they learn to give themselves to another person. One friend of mine said being in love was like "finally being at home with yourself." A romantic relationship guided by God, kept in sync by his Spirit and marked by the love of Christ is fulfilling, not fitful. It is self-giving, not self-absorbing.

Lasting love seeks the good of the other, no matter how this may affect the time spent with this person. Lasting love also longs for the joys of being together even when separation is necessary. One way to evaluate the depth of a romantic relationship is to consider how you feel when you are apart. Whether Breck and I are apart a work day, a weekend or longer, we can't wait to see each other. Actually we have to wait, like all people, but we love to see each other again—and the sooner the better. This longing to be together is natural for two people who love each other. It is a mature longing when times of separation are marked by excellent work, creative energy and thoughtful friendships with others.

Paula and Stan

Sometimes I find that the independent spirit promoted in our culture, country and churches leads to an attempt by earnest Christians not to "need" another person. The idea is embraced that pictures the best disciple as a "lone ranger," a person singularly immersed in the work God wants done.

I remember a time when a young woman wanted to talk about her relationship with a young man. Paula and Stan had

had a good friendship for several years. Over about a year and a half they had developed a serious romantic relationship and were considering a lifelong commitment. Paula wanted to know, "How do you know if it is real love?"

I knew Stan pretty well, but I asked Paula to tell me about him. I wanted to listen to how she talked about him. I wanted to know the focus of her attraction. I needed to hear her relate the story of their romance. In the course of talking about their relationship in response to my questions, Paula mentioned that Stan would be gone all summer. His teaching internship in special education was in another state. She was ready to graduate from nursing school and would stay home, work and take her state board examination. This was related in a very matter-of-fact tone and without a hint of regret over being separated for three months.

Since Paula's initial inquiry was how to know if you are really in love, I was concerned at her apparent lack of longing for Stan's company. I said at one point, "Oh, Paula, I'm sorry Stan has to be gone all summer. It will be such a long summer for you both!"

She reassured me that all this was God's will and that they both had plenty to do. "We'll be fine. It's not that long."

After this comment, I took a deep breath and said, "Well, Paula, God's will is always good. And I think this summer is in fact God's will for each of you. I'm not sure with this lack of longing that you are ready for engagement. I'm not sure this is lifelong love."

Paula's face fell, and she spoke very quickly. "Oh, I didn't think it would be right to miss Stan so much. I thought that would mean I wasn't trusting the Lord. Isn't it wrong to miss a person so much? To tell you the truth, I am dreading our time apart, and so is Stan. But we want to be obedient to God's will and work for us above all else."

I smiled at this unrestrained and honest confession of hormones, humanity and holiness. They are not mutually exclusive! "Paula," I said, "obedience is doing the right thing. And obedience doesn't always feel great. It's right, but sometimes it's hard. That's okay. That is even part of what it means to be a 'living *sacrifice.'* "I went on to tell about the times Breck and I are separated as a result of being obedient to God's will in ministry. We make the right choice and long for each other's company the whole time. When we are apart some distance, we almost always talk daily by phone. I reassured Paula that part of love is longing for the other person. One difference between true love and immature infatuation is the willingness to serve the other person at your own cost.

Paula was relieved to know that her honest dread of the long summer apart from Stan was a cause not for repentance but for thanksgiving. Their willingness to spend time apart to prepare professionally for a future together was obedience. The fact that they ached with longing for the summer to go quickly was love.

That conversation took place quite awhile ago on a sandy beach in the Florida Panhandle. Stan and Paula and their children are now an ocean away on the mission field, continuing to be obedient and in love. Today they often long for family, friends and the familiar. Then Paula and Stan remember one long, obedient summer that God used to teach them what real love was.

Allan and Michelle

I remembered Stan and Paula's story when I met recently with a couple for premarital counseling. It had been about ten years since Paula and I sat on the beach and talked, but I had seen the same willingness to sacrifice time, embrace longing and be obedient in these two young people. Michelle and Allan have worked hard on their relationship. They both come from broken homes and want their marriage to be right and solid. This was the first time we had met together in some time, so they enjoyed catching me up on the development of their relationship, their engagement and plans for a wedding a few months away.

As they finished their story, I couldn't miss their delight in each other and how far they had come in learning to love and serve each other. Their early relationship had been marked by some struggle with trusting each other when apart and not being possessive when together. When Allan and Michelle first began to date, I had had some doubts if their relationship would develop the maturity needed for a healthy marriage.

I smiled at this couple in love and told them how much I thought they had learned along the way. I told them when I first felt they would be all right: the summer Michelle went overseas on a short-term mission. I recalled how this was something she had wanted to do for some time and how I had seen Allan encourage her participation and commitment.

Allan said with enthusiasm, "Oh, yes! I knew how much Michelle wanted to do it. It was lonely for both of us, but so good for her. I wanted her to go. And the time apart was good for us. We got to know each other in a different way. We wrote letters and thought about things. We read a book together while apart. In fact, I think you recommended that to us!" Michelle agreed that the time had been valuable for maturing their relationship, building trust and recognizing how much they really did need and love each other.

Seasons of time within a friendship or romantic relationship are important to recognize. Trusting each other with time apart is important for making the most of the time you are together. Being faithful, thoughtful and honest with each other during times together makes the deep longing of love valuable when you are apart.

Time is entirely a gift of God's grace. True love unwraps this gift with prayer, patience and thanksgiving.

8

Touch Me,
Touch Me Not

THE GRAND CANYON can be a lot like true love between
a woman and a man. Consider the canyon. It looks different
from distinct vantage points. The north rim and south rim are
opposites, and without either one there would not be a canyon
at all. Each vista has a distinct beauty depending on the time,
weather and season. The canyon is exhilarating to explore, yet
potentially dangerous if its depth and width are not respected.
People have been lost and hurt. Some have fallen from great
heights; others have not survived the trek to the bottom. Crossing the gulf safely between the two is not easy. And it is not
safe if the hike is taken by the ill-prepared or reckless. What
the Grand Canyon needs to span the gap between the north
rim and the south rim and afford a magnificent view is a good
bridge.

Similarly, a man and woman in love have their individual
assets and liabilities. Their love is an adventure that can be
beautiful—and dangerous. A lot depends on the kind of bridge
between them.

If sex is a communication link spanning the canyon, the bridge many people use looks like a row of rotting boards set between two tattered ropes. It resembles the perilous swinging bridge in adventure films. Only heroes and heroines make it across; everybody else falls to their death. Enemies on both sides try to destroy the bridge and put an end to the crossing all together. Just getting to the other side becomes the quest. No one has time to enjoy the crossing itself, let alone to take in the view. Sex in the nineties is often a matter of bodily survival, not of enjoying beautiful scenery or deep satisfaction.

This flimsy adventure-film bridge is a Hollywood favorite. Danger is made to look thrilling. What we really see in the movies are stunt people taking all the risks; the real stars are too valuable. This is because real danger is not thrilling, it is threatening. The adventure-film bridge is not fun; it is fantasy. It's a fake pretending to be the real thing.

A *good* bridge over the canyon would have guardrails. The limits imposed by the guardrails would create immeasurable freedom. Crossing this bridge would be truly thrilling. Enjoying the view would be part of the adventure. The journey itself would become a source of joy, not just making it to the other side. Pleasure, not peril, would be the hallmark of the experience. Care would be taken to guard both sides of the canyon from enemies seeking to damage or destroy the bridge. Inspections would be regular, and standards would be set by the engineer who designed the bridge. Satisfaction, not survival, would become the cause for celebration.

Guardrails Create Freedom

We can enjoy the experience and the beauty of the canyon from a potentially perilous bridge if sturdy guardrails are provided. Likewise, the physical expressions of a romantic relationship need guardrails. Some of these rails are the immovable standards set by God the original Creator, our Engineer.

As the original designer of our sexuality God knows how grand the experience can be. Scripture provides a substantial blueprint for a safe bridge. It also provides the original map of the canyon and helps give an idea of the distinct views from both the "North and South rims." Because of course men and women think of sex differently!

Some guardrails are only in place for a time or for a particularly perilous season. Touch, like talk and time, needs to progress as the relationship reaches mutually held levels of commitment. Physical expressions of affection within a relationship need to be carefully considered, clearly communicated and closely guarded. Appropriate touch also needs to be enjoyed and appreciated as a part of what it means to be human beings loved by the Creator.

We should not be afraid of sex—"crossing the canyon." We should be careful where we stand and how and when we travel, and take it nice and slow. We should respect its potential dangers and be careful, not reckless. Many Christians are afraid of the journey. On the other hand, many Christians don't think they need guardrails. The former stand well back from the edge, never appreciating the depth and width and beauty of the adventure. The latter venture forth too quickly, ill-prepared and disrespectful of the canyon's power, and are hurt along the way.

Creators and Creative Authority

"The fear of the LORD is the beginning of knowledge" (Proverbs 1:7) and will help make us wise in the stewardship of God's good gifts to us. This fear is a deep respect with reverent awe that comes from a confidence that the Maker is right about how things that he has made work best. God is the original designer of sex, a powerful human appetite. Our wisdom about sexuality and conduct begins when we believe God to be the authority over its function and use.

I've heard a story that illustrates this well. A young man in the early days of automobiles was having trouble with his Model T Ford. The car was on the side of an old dirt road, and no matter what the young man did, it wouldn't start. An elderly man with a cane and slow walk came along and offered to help. The young man politely declined the old guy's offer with an attitude of "Thanks, but no thanks." The older fellow shook his head, mentioned what he thought the problem was from the sounds the car made, and began to pass on his way. He stopped after going just a short distance and called back some advice on how to get the car started.

The young man thought to himself, *What can this old guy know about fixing a car? He's probably never even ridden in one.* He tinkered for a few minutes, kicked the tires, cursed and then tried what the man had suggested. He was amazed when the car started right up! He drove off down the road and overtook the old man as he continued his walk. With a new respect, he thanked the man for his advice and then asked him, "So when did you come to know so much about cars?"

And the old guy smiled and said matter-of-factly, "Well, son, my name is Henry Ford, and I made that car."

The Creator-Inventor of human persons knows what's best for us. God knows how we are to run. The Lord knows how to redeem what we have broken. We are God's "Model T," broken and powerless to be who we are supposed to be. And God comes to us and gives us his Word, directions for repair, instructions for our well-being. Wisdom begins when we fear the Lord, listen well to his wisdom and obey his commands.

Returning to the illustration of the Grand Canyon bridge, this means paying attention to the Engineer who designed the bridge. Follow the rules. Enjoy. Be careful. Enjoy. Go slowly and at the right seasons for travel. Enjoy. Don't try to redesign the bridge. Enjoy. Stay on the bridge; don't jump off or try a shorter route. Don't travel across with a stranger. It's a good bridge.

And it's a potentially dangerous bridge. Pay attention.

Rudy and Karen

Some have gone ahead on their own makeshift adventure without knowing about God's guardrailed bridge but then heard about it during the journey. Some have managed to return safely to a starting point and discover for themselves the Engineer's good bridge. It's possible to learn how to make the crossing wisely and not miss the beauty. Rudy Carson started off a lot like this.

Rudy set off for college with a scholarship, an old sedan and a stack of condoms. The state university he would attend was the "number-one party school" in the country, and he intended to join the party. Safely, of course. He wanted to graduate and didn't want to get totally wasted and drop out as his cousin had done a few years before.

Rudy set off on a few short hikes down the canyon road, but every trail seemed to loop around into a dead end. Rudy would get so far, have some fun, maybe make love to a young woman and end up feeling pretty dissatisfied. The party wasn't all it was promoted to be.

A few things happened to bring Rudy back to the canyon's edge, a level place to restart his journey across the sexual canyon. He met some men and women who had found real security and freedom by crossing the canyon on a guardrailed bridge. He met some fellow students who were taking it nice and slow across the bridge. They knew the Engineer personally. One of these careful travelers was really beautiful. Her name was Karen.

Rudy became a Christian in the middle of his first semester at "Party U." He had never had a friendship with a woman like Karen. She was fully committed to the lordship of Christ in her life. She trusted the guardrails of Scripture. Her friendship with Rudy had boundaries and dynamics that he didn't understand.

Rudy drew me aside after a campus fellowship meeting one evening and wanted to talk. He began the conversation by saying, "I need to know the rules. I really like Karen. I've had sex before and never felt about a woman what I feel about Karen. I haven't even touched Karen, and I care for her so much! I may even love her. I don't know for sure, but I need to know what is okay and what is not okay. You know I haven't been a Christian long, and I am beginning to realize things are really different."

I was stunned by Rudy's eagerness, sincerity and honesty. I reassured him that the conduct of God's family is quite distinct from that of Party U. That day we began to talk, and our conversations have continued—even after Rudy and Karen eventually made a safe and joyful crossing together.

It was a pleasure to see Rudy understand for the first time that God is not embarrassed by the sexuality of his creation. Rudy felt better knowing that sex was God's idea. Rudy felt worse knowing how he had misused, even abused, his own sexuality. He was impressed to learn that he was marked by the image of God. And he was embarrassed to confess how he had so casually vandalized that image. He grew to understand the simultaneous sorrow and joy of being a sinner and having a Savior.

Rudy wanted to honor God with a new way of living a new life in God's family. Karen seemed to know the conduct rules of the kingdom, and he didn't. I suppose I was Rudy's tour guide for his Grand Canyon bridge crossing. Some of the information I passed on made a lot of sense to Rudy. Other bits of guidance surprised him, and we had to confirm the truth of the advice in the Engineer's manual—Scripture. Sometimes Rudy would respond, "You're kidding, right?" And other times, "You were right, and I'm not kidding!" Through it all Karen and Rudy found that sexuality and holiness are not mutually exclusive.

Sexual and Holy

It is possible to learn to love without lust and touch without transgression. It is possible to transform frustration into self-control. Hormones don't have to be the enemy of holiness. Friday nights and Sunday mornings can be equally sanctified. Sex can be grand, the canyon can be crossed and God can be glorified. He is always glorified when we honor his desire and design for us.

God's desire, as well as his design, is that in sexual union two shall become one (Genesis 2:24), not just physically but spiritually and emotionally as well. Sexual union is a physical expression of two people's complete vulnerability to each other. It is safeguarded and blessed only in a covenant relationship—marriage. Physical union can certainly take place outside the marriage relationship, but vulnerability outside the boundaries of covenantal security is unhealthy to body and soul. This is reflected clearly in the teaching of Jesus on adultery and divorce (Matthew 5:31–32; 19:9; Mark 10:11–12; Luke 16:18).

Marriage is a heterosexual and monogamous lifelong union between two people who establish a home distinct from that of their parents. It's "leaving and cleaving" (see Genesis 2:24 KJV). A married couple may move upstairs to a separate room or around the world to a different country, but a new primary family unit is created. This union is legalized, celebrated and recognized in different ways by different cultural, traditional and religious ceremonies. A major reason for a wedding is to notify the community that the sexual relationship between these two people is exclusive and not to be violated.

Intimate sexual expression in any form without this commitment leads to emotional as well as physical fornication. This kind of involvement, unaccompanied by an equal, lifelong commitment from both parties, breaks hearts, frustrates relationships and can destroy health.

When dating, people need to know where they are in a relationship to determine the extent of physical affection that is a godly reflection of their degree of commitment to each other. Different couples bring different histories to a dating relationship, and people will need different paces for romantic courtship to define their own obedience to God in areas not clearly dealt with in Scripture. Some couples can enjoy a lingering embrace without temptation, and others cannot. People are different, but it is generally inappropriate to kiss on a first date, or to never have kissed before your honeymoon!

As with the issues of talk and time, speaking the truth in love concerning touch is of great importance. Permission must be mutually given (verbally or nonverbally) for physical expressions of affection to be shared. If there is any doubt at all about its intention or reception, then ask. Talk about it. It can save a lot of pain, misunderstanding and heartbreak.

Gwen and Gary

Breck and I are friends with a young married couple who had a careful and slowly progressing courtship. They talked about every new advance in their physical relationship very clearly— with good reason. Gwen had been raped during her first year at a community college. Since that incident, she had had a difficult time even being in the same room with any man she did not know. It took time for her to begin to trust herself and not feel helpless in certain situations. It took time for her even to begin to believe that other men would not treat her in the same way. For two years she had not told anyone.

When she transferred to the university, she'd made excuses not to date at all. She wouldn't let young men in the Christian fellowship walk her back to her apartment alone. She drew back from brotherly hugs given by those she knew in her small-group Bible study.

Gwen finally told her story to her roommate, and her roommate came with her to talk to me. From then on Gwen began to work toward her healing and began to recognize that she needed to learn to trust God and others again. She deepened her spiritual life, grew as a disciple and talked things out with a professional counselor.

She began to allow friendships to grow between her and her brothers in Christ. During the last semester of her senior year, Gwen was healed enough to share her story with the campus fellowship. Many people began to understand her for the first time. A few men in the fellowship saw that Gwen hadn't been aloof or cold; she had been injured and alienated.

During graduate school, Gwen met a young man named Gary. He lived a distance from where she attended graduate school and asked if he could write. She was hesitant but did allow the correspondence to begin. Several months and lots of letters later, they began to go out of their way to see each other during conferences, travels and holiday breaks. During one of these visits Gwen told Gary what she had gone through and explained that she would need time to grow into a relationship or trust any expression of affection between them. Gary listened well and was careful in his conduct and care for Gwen.

He asked permission to hold her hand. He asked permission to put his arm around her. And slowly but surely Gary and Gwen began a true love relationship that continues today in marriage.

There was one point in their courtship, as they neared the time to discuss the commitment to lifelong love, that Gwen asked me to help her convince Gary that she was much better and he really could linger in his kisses a bit! She had tried to reassure him but thought maybe I could help. Gary had been very thoughtful and careful, but he had no problem complying with this encouragement.

Today, nearly one in every four women has been the victim of some sort of sexual assault. It is wise to take the same care, work on the same communication and extend the same understanding to any person. The physical and sexual history of people is often unknown, even between pretty good friends. Discretion is more than the better part of valor when it comes to expressions of affection in a developing relationship. Discretion is also a smart way to guard your heart, respect your brother or sister in Christ and avoid physical, as well as emotional, fornication.

Safeguards for Sexual Conduct

I get a lot of questions about sexual conduct from those who come to me for advice and help. What constitutes "intimate sexual expression"? What kinds of behavior should be left for the security and freedom of marriage? Are there any exceptions? How can I avoid doing something I may regret if a romance doesn't work out?

To help answer these questions, I usually outline four clear-cut rules that I think are faithful to the prohibitions of Scripture concerning sexual intercourse outside of marriage. They help keep romance in the relationship, while establishing mutually acknowledged boundaries to help resist sexual temptation. It is wise to agree on limits of time, talk and touch at every stage of a romantic relationship *before* the need for them arises. It is much harder to think clearly, assert your will or slow things down in the middle of increasing passion. Human sexual appetite is too powerful to trust to a see-what-to-do-as-we-go-along strategy.

This quote from Charlotte Brontë's novel *Jane Eyre* reflects well on a struggle that is not new to anyone:

Laws and principles are not for the times when there is no temptation: they are for such moments as this, when body and soul rise in mutiny against their rigour; stringent are they; inviolate they shall be. If at my individual convenience I might break them, what would be their worth?

We readily admit that other bodily appetites need control, and the "rules" of control are best set before the possibility of temptation is present. An athlete-in-training makes up his or her mind what to eat, what not to eat, how much to work out and rest before the weekend trip to Mama's home cooking. And winners stick to their rules. Hunger is a controllable appetite. It helps to have rules. You know what to avoid and say no to. You also know what to accept with thanksgiving and enjoy. You really enjoy one slice of Mama's apple pie because you already have made it clear one slice is all you can have.

Sex is another human appetite that is controllable. Sexual desire does not have to become lust, neither does it have to be immediately satisfied. Desire delayed until marriage is not desire denied but controlled. The rules I suggest are designed for controlling the appetite, enhancing holiness and creating some safety *and* freedom in a romantic relationship. Between the first date and the need for enforcing these rules there should be plenty of time for simple expressions of affection. These include hand-holding, caress-free embracing, brief kissing and nonerotic touching. These affectionate expressions should grow slowly and be mutually agreed on, whether consent is spoken or unspoken.

Rule 1: Four Feet on the Floor

If both people romantically involved remembered to keep all four feet on the floor during a date or a study break, it sure would be helpful. I have had more than a few students and young couples tell me how handy this rule was when they were so tempted to lie on the couch together, "just take naps" together or watch TV together. It's amazing how natural it feels to want to get a little more prone the more you fall in love and spend romantic time together. The appetite for sex is natural. But self-control is a fruit of God's spirit, and keeping four feet on the floor is one practical way to practice self-control.

A couple came to my office on campus awhile back. Rachel

and Miguel were holding hands, and both were grinning from ear to ear. I said, "What's up?"

They smiled even more broadly and squeezed hands, and Rachel said joyfully, "You will be so proud of us!"

Miguel nodded vigorously and said, "Yes, last night, we were sitting on the couch—"

"Just watching TV," Rachel inserted and continued, "and I found myself picking up my feet to sorta lay against Miguel—"

"And I really wanted her to do this, really," confessed Miguel, "but suddenly I saw her feet on the couch and remembered 'four on the floor'!" They both laughed.

Rachel continued, "Yes, Miguel just looked at me, and I knew what he was thinking. So I sat up and said, 'Okay, four on the floor.' I have to admit at first I wondered if this wasn't silly, but then—you tell her, Miguel."

"Well, we sat there for a while, kinda unhappy. I got to thinking to myself how much I just want Rachel sometimes, like all the way. I started thinking things. And then, like all of a sudden, I saw that's what this was all about. These rules you told us probably kept us from stuff we really don't want to get into, not really."

"Yes," Rachel added. "When Miguel told me what he had been thinking—well, I had no real idea how tempted he was at times. I thought it was a little thing, but to him it could have been really difficult."

"Anyway," said Miguel, "thanks for the rules. I have to say when I first heard them and I wasn't dating, I thought they were pretty weird. But with Rachel—well, I need all the help I can get. We don't want to mess up. I didn't think I would be so tempted since I became a Christian, but I am."

"Yeah, that's what I thought," said Rachel. "We wanted to drop by and ask you to pray for us and to let you know that this stuff really works."

Rachel and Miguel are fictional names, like all the names in this book, but the conversation was real and the story is accurate. Rachel and Miguel dated for some time, grew apart one summer, decided not to continue romantically and are still friends. There were some difficult conversations and decisions as their relationship changed, but very few regrets. They both wanted to trust the Lord with their lives, and their personal goals and interests just grew apart. They were both very grateful that their commitment to sexual restraint spared them from the painful regrets and consequences that were the experience of some of their friends.

Rule 2: No Clothes Off

It's really helpful to keep blouses buttoned, pants zipped and erotic body parts covered. Makes sense, doesn't it? Well, it does now while you are reading this book, sitting up with your feet on the floor. But there may be times when the thought of touching some skin or having some skin touched drives every other thought from your mind. Keeping your clothes on is a good rule to have. Rule 2 has the same sort of accountable helpfulness that rule 1 affords. The no–clothes–off rule sets a limit, a concrete limit, that can remind you to cooperate with the Spirit's desire and gift of self–control.

Along with the no–clothes–off rule, it's a good idea to not slip your hands under each other's clothing. Yes, it's possible to keep your clothes on, keeping the "letter of the law," while doing plenty to not keep the "spirit of the law"! So don't untuck each other's shirts and feel around for what's underneath. Leave bras hooked, pants zipped and shirttails tucked in.

If we care for each other, our clothing should reflect our intentions, not our temptations. Men and women of God should dress thoughtfully. The dress code of the kingdom is chaste and modest. Women need to remember that men are more sexually stimulated by visual means than they are. Women need to dress modestly to minimize the stimulation men receive, especially from the exposure of breasts and upper thighs. Men are certainly responsible for their own conduct, but women need to take into consideration the temptation tendencies of the opposite sex.

A couple called me and had to talk "right away." Butler and Diane had been friends for quite some time, had begun to date when Butler was in his senior year of college, and were nearing the point of engagement. They needed to tell me about something that had happened in the car during their trip to Butler's hometown to visit his folks for the weekend. Diane had fallen asleep as Butler drove. She woke up suddenly when she felt his hand slip between her legs. She jumped, yelled and hardly spoke to him the rest of the weekend. He couldn't believe how stupid the whole thing was, but he kept his distance and tried to apologize at every opportunity.

Diane was really angry. She confided in her roommate when she returned. Her roommate said, "Dump the bum! How dare he make a move like that!" Butler was apologetic, embarrassed and confused. It had been his idea to come and talk to me. Diane had agreed. She didn't know what to think. She felt she still loved Butler, but this had thrown her for a loop. She was asking herself how well she really knew him.

We sat down, and they proceeded to tell me the story. Diane did most of the talking. Butler kept saying "I'm sorry" with every comment he made. His summary of the incident went something like this: "I don't know what made me do it. Diane fell asleep, and there were her legs. I just wanted to touch her. I know I shouldn't have. We have been really good—really. Something just came over me, and there was my hand, and she woke up, and I am so sorry. I really want her to forgive me. I hope she can. It won't happen again. I'm so sorry. I promise, I really mean it."

I agreed with his confession and confirmed the wrongness of his intimate touch. Butler was wrong. He had no excuse for what he did. So we were all in agreement. Diane had every right to be angry. Now what? She wanted to forgive him, but she needed some encouragement that this would not happen again.

At this point I asked Butler what he felt was the genesis of the temptation. When did he "first spy the apple," so to speak?

"Well, it was her legs. She had on these short shorts," he said, and continued quickly, "I know that this is no excuse for what I did, but I hope she doesn't wear those shorts again."

I looked at Diane, who stared at Butler in amazement. "Really?" she said. "You know I don't think I have very good legs—I'm too skinny. I didn't know you'd think things like that about my legs!"

"Oh, yeah," Butler assured her. "You'd be surprised."

I then asked Diane what she thought about this revelation. She said she wouldn't wear short shorts again and told Butler to tell her if anything else really tempted him. He needed to keep his hands to himself, but she didn't want to make it more difficult.

We talked for some time about the sexual stimulation differences between men and women. Diane and Butler made some new rules for themselves. Diane decided to forgive Butler and determined to be more thoughtful in how she dressed. She also began to realize that she was more sexually powerful and attractive than she had ever thought. Diane told me later, "I'm convinced there are reasons to be modest, even for a skinny, flat-chested girl like me!"

No clothes off. And be modest in the clothes you have on.

Rule 3: No Erotic Fondling

Some places on our bodies tend to be more easily stimulated sexually than others. These places certainly include the genitals, but there are more areas to consider in rule 3. Breasts, necks, thighs and earlobes are top contenders for places to avoid in fingertip and kissing exploration.

Some people also have other sensitive areas that need to be off-limits for them. How do you handle these individual idiosyncrasies? You speak the truth in love: "I don't know why touching my elbow like that does what it does to me, but it does. So don't."

I remember from ages ago—some junior-high school talk when boys were told why not to throw girls in the pool ("What if they are having their period?")—that we girls were told not to sit in a boy's lap. I also remember ignoring this advice generally. Because I was the skinniest girl in the Western Hemisphere, I usually got picked to be the lap-sitter in a too-full car. I also remember my shock at being pretty much dumped on the floor once as my classmate became "uncomfortable." I didn't catch on right away that he had been stimulated, just by touch—not desire—and had begun to have an erection. He just shoved me off his lap! Looking back on this prehistoric incident, I realize the poor guy must have been so embarrassed.

Adult human beings are sexually responsive—men more by sight, women more by touch. More than a few times brotherly hugs are offered without a sexual agenda at all, and "sisters" don't think of the man like their "brother" at all! If women need to be extra-thoughtful about how they dress, men need to be more thoughtful about how they touch. When in doubt, *ask!*

A Christian brother's concern for a sister at church or on campus may look and sound something like this: "I'm sorry to hear about the return of your mom's cancer. Here's a tissue for your nose. I would like to hug you, you know, comfort you— that's my only intention. Is that okay?" Speak the truth in love. It helps everyone stay clear, receive what is really being offered, relax and act like the family of God. Be thoughtful with even the most innocent of touches.

Less than innocent touching, erotic fondling, is completely off-limits prior to marriage. I have had dating couples who are "virgins" come for help with an increasingly frustrating habit that they can't get under control: mutual masturbation. They haven't had "intercourse," but they rub and fondle each other, usually until the man ejaculates. I've had Christians ask me if this is "okay" because it helps them release sexual tension so they don't "do it."

They have done it. They have penetrated each other's minds and deep emotional feelings and have manipulated each other's wills. The sexual organs may not have fully joined, but they are not emotionally, psychologically or physically pure. Virginity is an issue of personal holiness, not just physical wholeness—whether a woman's hymen is intact or whether a man's penis has entered a woman's body.

With the increasing social acceptance of premarital sex comes a depersonalization of sexual intercourse. Our language mirrors this change. The King James biblical language reflects the Hebrew idea of a man "knowing" his wife. It indicated an intimacy full of personal knowledge—of the soul as well as the body. To penetrate a woman was to "know" her. The word for "know" in the Old Testament, *yāḏa'*, was used of God's knowledge of human beings and creation (Genesis 18:19; Psalm 50:11; Isaiah 48:8). In certain contexts it means the knowledge of a skill or the ability to distinguish between things. *Yāḏa'* acknowledged that the act of intercourse was personal as well as penetrating. There is something more than physical that is communicated, touched, and known between two people who are sexually intimate.

In my own lifetime sexual "knowing" was at one time called "intercourse," which still alludes to some sort of communication beyond the physical. This has given way to the "making love" of the sexual revolution of the sixties. Typical of my generation, what you "feel" is all that counts. So less connection is acknowledged. "Knowing" is limited to "feeling."

This has given way to the consumer-age, what-you-get-out-of-it performance focus reflected in the expression "Do it." Just do it. The language of love is no longer personal; it's a program, a promotion. Sex is something you "do," not a part of who you are—not even in terms of what a person might feel.

No erotic fondling. Rule 3 may actually help make sex something to look forward to instead of something to be taken for granted or feared. The truly exciting and stimulating might return. For a postmodern and bored world of "been there, done that," the wonder of sexuality needs to be reexplored. Awe needs to be added to education. Waiting for what you desire increases a sense of value in what you anticipate. Sexual affection needs to be extended slowly, carefully, thoughtfully and humanly.

Rule 4: No French Kissing

This is actually a subset of rule 3. The tongue is definitely an erotic organ. Dating couples need to keep their own tongues behind their own teeth. No, I'm not kidding. Yes, I am serious. And despite what Hollywood, MTV and the surrounding world promotes, there is more to a simple kiss than many let themselves appreciate. I think it is interesting that in two fairly recent movies, the intimacy of kissing has been rated as higher than that of genital intercourse. In *Pretty Woman,* the Julia Roberts character tells the Richard Gere character that kissing is "special" and that it's reserved for true love. In the movie ironically titled *French Kiss,* the Kevin Kline character confesses much the same idea to the character played by Meg Ryan. In both movies the point the character makes highlights the modern emotional vacuum of genital sex and is an attempt to recover the intimacy of romance itself.

No French kissing. It is an act of penetration. It is generally very effective in physically preparing the body for genital intercourse. If you are not married and cannot follow through on the latter, then it is not wise to increase the sexual tension of your bodies.

Avoiding Frustration

Many Christians only focus on the major prohibition regarding sexual intercourse before or outside of marriage. They consider anything up to that point within the boundaries and acceptable conduct. This can be like sitting obediently at a stoplight with the accelerator pushed to the floor, the RPMs in the red zone and the car's engine overheating.

It is wise to remember that as human beings we have the capacity to learn habitual somatic responses to physical stimuli. Certain mental, emotional or physical stimuli, when repeated, can cause certain other set responses of the body. For example, thinking about your favorite dessert may make your mouth water. Smokers who are trying to quit are strongly encouraged to disrupt their routines, even rearrange furniture. They need to disconnect from even the remotest routine associated with smoking.

My husband and I have helped counsel couples with sexual dysfunction that manifested itself *after* marriage because the physical habits while dating created a learned bodily response that was not immediately reversed by vows and wedding rings. Premature ejaculation for men and the lack of orgasm in women are two of the more frequent consequences. Learned frustration—sitting at the stoplight with the accelerator to the floor—is avoidable.

Premarital sex is junk food for the body. It's the snack-food of the soul. It may taste sweet for a moment, but will kill an appetite for a balanced meal. Marriage provides a banquet of delight and deep satisfaction. A healthy appetite includes hunger. Desire delayed is not desire denied. Christians need not deny they have a sexual appetite, but do need to control the sexual appetite. Sexual snacking dulls the hunger and compromises holiness. It does not fit us for the long journey toward Eden.

Rules like these create freedom because they afford a measure of security in a potentially threatening situation. Sexual expression in a dating relationship can help prepare a couple for lifelong love. Or it can destroy lives as well as love. Using these guardrails can help you safely approach the good bridge over a beautiful canyon.

God is good. And sex, like the canyon, is grand. Journey in faith, and when the time is right, cross on the good bridge and enjoy.

9

Detours, Potholes,
Road Hazards

AFTER READING THE PREVIOUS chapter you might have
a few questions, most of them starting, "But what if..."

□ But what if I am no longer a virgin but want to wait until
I'm married from now on?

□ But what if I am a virgin and I get involved with someone
who isn't?

□ But what if I want to remain a virgin, but find the only
release for sexual tension to be masturbation?

□ But what if my girlfriend and I have gone "too far," but not
all the way, and want to back up and slow down?

□ But what if we've had sex and now want to wait until we're
married? Do we just pretend it never happened?

□ But what if we went too far just once and now find that we
don't really trust each other? We were fine, but now can't relax
at all—even just talking!

□ But what if I contracted an STD [a sexually transmitted
disease like herpes or gonorrhea] before I became a Christian?
When and how do I tell the person I am dating now?

☐ But what if I have never kissed anyone—never even had a date—and sometimes I wonder if there is something wrong with me?

☐ But what if I've grown up with a lot of pornography around—books, magazines and movies? I can't get certain images out of my head. Can I ever be "sexual and holy"?

☐ But what if I have experimented sexually—even with the same sex—and now that I know Christ, I want to live my life right?

All these questions essentially ask, "But what if I have a past and want a future? What do I do in the present?" These are all real questions that I have been asked before. Here are a few stories drawn from the lives of real people who asked them.

Hugh and Liza

I first met Hugh and Liza when they visited my office for some counseling. They came in holding hands and looking uncomfortable, and both seemed nervous. They had come to see me as a "third party." Hugh and Liza each went to different churches that taught the Word and honored the gospel. They had discussed their predicament with their pastors, who recommended they talk to me. Both Liza and Hugh felt good about this, since they were more confident that a person who didn't know them would be more "neutral" and they could each trust any advice, admonition or counsel more readily.

I greeted them warmly and tried to put them at ease. I expressed my respect for their pastors and then asked Hugh and Liza how each of them had come to know the Lord Jesus Christ. They were surprised that this was my first question. Frankly, I thought I had a pretty good guess what they had come to talk about. But I knew their salvation and standing with God had to be the first issue they discussed. No matter what they had come to deal with, they needed to hear themselves and each other confess out loud the really definitive truth of their lives. I am confident that the Savior is always greater than our sin, and I knew these two young people needed to share that confidence.

First John 3:20 reminds us that our hearts condemn us when our actions deny the truth we claim to know in the gospel, but that in spite of this very condemnation, "God is greater than our hearts, and he knows everything." Liza and Hugh had come to talk about sinful actions that denied who they were as confessing Christians. They needed to rehearse the reality of their faith before confessing their failure. So I listened to each tell their story of salvation.

How Did We End Up Here?

They had both been raised by parents who shared the Christian faith with them. Hugh and Liza had both had a real and personal relationship with Christ since grade-school days, and they had grown in their commitment to Christ through their adolescent years in biblically rich youth groups. When they came to the same college, they each joined a different Christian group on campus and were active in their respective churches. I was assured of the salvation they both confessed by their understanding of the gospel and the obvious contrition they felt over behavior that they knew dishonored God.

Next, I asked Liza and Hugh how they had come to know each other and how they had fallen in love. This caused them to smile, and they begin to relax a little more. This was important for me to see. Their gestures, their tone of voice and how they told their stories all indicated to me that Liza and Hugh weren't out to wound each other. They had not come to counseling to point fingers or place blame. They still liked each other, and they still wanted to be in love with each other. I listened intently and hopefully as they remembered the first time they met, what they liked about each other and how the relationship had deepened.

This rehearsal was important because after some disappointments and regrets in the relationship, they needed to be reminded how good it had been and could be. During this time, Liza and Hugh created hope for each other. It was good for Liza to hear how creative and insightful Hugh first found her to be. And Hugh needed to hear again how his music and his engaging way of interacting with others first caught Liza's attention. I asked them what they found especially wonderful about each other and what made this seem like "true love" as distinct from other romances in the past.

Liza and Hugh both found it easy to reflect on these things. Whatever difficulty or disobedience had brought them to this time had not completely overwhelmed their appreciation for each other, nor their sense of basic love for each other. This too was important for me to see and hear as their confidant and counselor. I had a feeling that they were heading for a time when they would have to say no to each other, and it was good for them to remember all that they could say yes to in their relationship. In fact, as they spoke about each other, I could sense that both Liza and Hugh felt that what had gone wrong threatened what they deeply valued in the relationship.

What Went Wrong?
At this point I told them that I needed to ask them why they needed to see me, but before they answered, I wanted to pray with them. We held hands as I voiced a prayer of thanksgiving and gratitude for the Lord's faithfulness to Liza and Hugh. I gave thanks for their salvation and the work of Jesus in the redemption of their lives. I then asked that we all be particularly aware of the Holy Spirit's presence, guidance, counsel and willingness to give wisdom as our conversation continued. I prayed that the Lord would continue to give Liza and Hugh clarity of thought, honest insight to their feelings and a willingness to believe God's good intention and way for them.

We then resumed the conversation; I asked, "So, specifically, why are you here to talk to me?" They both indicated that they were having trouble with their sexual restraint, but neither Liza nor Hugh was specific initially. They just said they needed some "accountability" because they couldn't be married for some time. Marriage was a possibility they had seriously explored, but they had concluded that this was not the right time. After listening to their story and reasons for delaying marriage, I understood their dilemma. This was not a situation where marriage was being put off for worldly or selfish reasons.

But Liza and Hugh needed help to get their physical relationship under control. I asked several questions in an attempt to get them to be more specific with what the problem was, but they found it difficult to talk about. Liza would look away, Hugh would go off on a tangent, and they both grew tense. These were two people caught in a situation that they'd never expected to be in. Their struggle was totally foreign to their expectations of themselves as Christians. They hemmed and hawed and talked around the issue.

I finally interrupted gently and asked them, "Are you virgins?" With a simultaneous expression of relief, they both answered together, "No!" They were so surprised by how loudly and firmly and instantly they both answered that they just turned and stared at each other.

After a moment to take in the depth of that confession, Hugh turned to me and said, "But we were virgins before each other. It's us."

Liza added, "And we didn't really mean for it to happen, but now, even when we say we won't, we go too far again."

As the confession continued I found that they had had sexual intercourse on a fairly regular basis for over six months. Neither of them had used birth control, because they never meant for it to happen again. Liza was not pregnant and had not been, but they both acknowledged that they were aware of the sexual roulette they risked in this regard. Both Hugh and Liza wanted to start over and completely slow down the sexual relationship. They had several good reasons, but didn't know how it could be done.

Why Was It So Wrong?

Their primary reason was a mutual belief that premarital sex disobeyed God. They had always intended to marry as virgins. They believed the authority of Scripture as well as the wisdom of their church teachings and traditions. Their secondary but more motivating reason was that this disobedience was proving to be a threat to the entire relationship. They were not as comfortable with each other. They found it difficult to talk honestly with each other. Even everyday conversation and planning seemed to be threatened by sexual lust and a lack of control. They reflected an underlying sense of fear and distrust. "I love Liza, but I feel so suspicious of myself whenever we are together. I don't want to think about what might happen, but it is always there, like a threat." "I want to be with Hugh, but before we meet, I almost dread it. I don't like feeling so fearful of being with Hugh. I love him, but I don't trust myself or him."

The physical intensity of the relationship had overwhelmed emotional trust, ruined meaningful conversation and disrupted their spiritual lives. Both Liza and Hugh felt like hypocrites in worship, found it hard to pray and avoided Bible study. They wanted help because sexual intimacy was making them strangers. To each other and to God. They were not happy, but they really were in love and valued their relationship. With each other and with God.

Hugh and Liza felt desperate, but not hopeless. Their faith in God and their knowledge of the forgiveness offered through the cross of Christ gave them a basic sense that there must be a way to start over. They were seriously heartbroken and injured by their sin, but in this "distant country" (Luke 15) they remembered what it might be like to go back home. Theologically they had an idea, but physically and emotionally they were mapless. They found themselves in a place where they'd never thought they would be and had no bearings or directions to begin the journey.

Which Way Is Home?

My counsel started with a physical map. First, I talked to them about the need for both of them to be willing to go through this together, talk it out every step of the way and be absolutely honest with me about success and failure on the journey. They readily agreed. Then I let them know that it could be really hard on them. This was not a one-night slip (that's difficult enough), but their fully intimate sexual conduct had gone on for some time. The habits of lust would be more difficult for their bodies to unlearn because of this. Therefore, the starting point for their new behavior would have to be radical, to really disrupt their habits. Would they trust my advice and go for it? A bit more soberly, they agreed.

They found the four rules outlined in the previous chapter helpful. They were like the four points of a compass on the map. Hugh asked me to write them down. They were relieved. I could sense how these guardrails would create some safety for this couple. (In the next few weeks this safety would begin to rebuild a trust that was less naive.) Both Hugh and Liza agreed that the rules made a lot of sense and would have given them some logical markers that might have helped if they had had them earlier.

Then we talked about where to begin an obedient and healthy sense of constraint. If these rules were an outer limit, where was the starting point for Liza and Hugh? This relationship had been so wounding to each of them, and so long-standing, I knew they needed to *literally* start over. They had at least eighteen months until marriage was an option. And even if they could have married much sooner, the turmoil and disappointment they felt at this time would have carried over into marriage. If they could take the next eighteen months to heal and learn some healthier habits of relationship and romance, then they would take less negative emotional, sexual and spiritual baggage into their marriage.

Taking a deep breath and praying a fervent prayer, I said, "Now, for this week, I want you to meet each other again. It will be hard, but I want you to 'pretend' to get to know each other. This week I would like you to be exceptionally polite. 'Please,' 'thank you,' 'you're welcome.' You need to create a just-getting-to-know-you atmosphere. This may sound crazy, but re-creating 'verbal virginity' can remind you of your long-term intentions and what it will take to recapture a godly romance."

Hugh and Liza looked at each other and smiled. "Does this make sense?" I asked. Liza responded immediately and said to Hugh, "Yeah, and when you call, you have to see *if* I can go out." She laughed and said, "I'll say 'yes,' but you have to ask!"

Hugh reached out and took Liza's hand and nodded his agreement. They suddenly let go of each other's hands and looked at me, and Hugh asked for both of them, "Oh! Can we hold hands?"

I smiled at these two humbled and willing students and said, "Well, if you really only knew each other a week, I'd say no, but let's make sure we keep *grace* and *truth* both fully working in redeeming this relationship. Hold hands, but don't rub fingers, okay?"

Liza and Hugh both looked a bit uncomfortable with my candor, but they knew they could tell me anything.

Avoiding Pitfalls and Detours

The last thing we did during this first meeting was discuss what situations or other things Hugh and Liza felt contributed to their lack of sexual self-control. Liza offered that they mostly got carried away when they were alone in Hugh's apartment. Hugh said he felt weakest when he was stressed with school-work or time pressures. I asked them to suggest ways to avoid these contributing factors. Liza said she would have to leave when Hugh's roommate or another friend wasn't there. It would be hard, but they both acknowledged that being alone was a problem.

I agreed, of course, and was glad to see the extent of their willingness to draw lines for themselves. I affirmed the wisdom of seeing this problem and asked one extra thing in this regard: Hugh and Liza each needed to tell their roommates about this aspect of their accountability. The roommates didn't need to know the extent of Liza's and Hugh's involvement, but if they knew there was a basic problem, they would be more likely to let Liza and Hugh know when they would be around and when they would be leaving. Anticipating a schedule would enhance compliance with this discipline.

Hugh readily agreed. His roommate was a Christian and would respect the effort. Liza lived in a sorority house. Her roommate, as well as other women in the house, was sexually active and might think Liza was being stupid. Liza had enough pressure in the living situation as a Christian and didn't want to tell her roommate. So I asked her for another accountability suggestion—someone who knew her schedule pretty well and whom she could confide in. She really couldn't think of anyone. (Later on we talked about how her other friendships had been significant casualties of her consuming relationship with Hugh.) At this point I asked Liza to think about it and to pray for new female friendships to develop. I told them both, "In the meantime, don't see each other alone."

For the stress and school tension as contributing factors, I reassured them that physical and emotional tiredness always compromises the energy needed for self-control. Besides taking care of themselves physically (rest, exercise and a good diet), I asked them to tell each other when they felt this pressure. "Like, during midterms you may just have to not see each other at all. You may have to see absence as a gift you are willing to give each other to protect and care for each other." I assured them that we would take it one step at a time and try not to overreact or underreact to specific situations or temptations. We would meet weekly and pray "without ceasing."

The Possibility of Restoration

We ended our meeting as all three of us prayed for God's restoration and strength and wisdom. I remember continuing in prayer for a time after Liza and Hugh left. It would be so hard for them. I had helped other couples "back up and start over" after single or brief episodes of sexual sin, but this couple had been entrenched in a physically satisfying relationship. They both admitted deep desire. This was one time I was glad of Scripture's assurance that doing "all things" is possible in the strength of Christ (Philippians 4:13 KJV). I prayed for Hugh and Liza to know the power of Christ in this of all things.

As in all the stories told in this book, the names and certain details have been changed, but in a journal I have this recorded concerning the story of "Liza and Hugh":

Liza and Hugh are really doing well! They have kept "the rules" and repented well when they got too close to breaking even these! I am so grateful that they have been determined to be honest with me. About three weeks into this renewal of chastity Hugh came to see me alone. He began by saying, "You know this may sound weird, but I sense almost a joy in waiting—isn't that weird?"

I think he was honestly afraid that he was not normal anymore. I assured him, no it was not "weird," but indeed joy is the norm for God's people. God alone knows what is best and good. This joy is what God desired all along and what their previous conduct denied them. Out of his grace, God is allowing Liza and Hugh to rediscover and reclaim what they had forfeited in sin. The Lord is returning that which the "locust" of sin had taken away. God is good. How I praise him for his redemptive work and mercy. Lord, help them make it!

Liza and Hugh did make it. They were married about eighteen months later, more in love with each other and right with God. They are a couple who can tell you they agree with Hebrews 12:11: "No discipline seems pleasant at the time, but painful. Later on, however, it produces a harvest of righteousness and peace for those who have been trained by it." By God's immeasurable grace, even a touch of joy is possible! Edging toward Eden is possible even from a long way off.

Backing up and starting over can be done. Depending on the extent and duration of intimacy, select a radically new starting point physically. This point should be specific ("yes, we can hold hands, but not rub fingers"), and this point should be a significant distance from the intimacy boundaries that have been crossed. It isn't commonly helpful to back up just a little bit, because the penultimate intimacy is a big part of the problem. For instance, if the temptation to fondle a woman's breasts is the intimacy boundary crossed, making a rule to keep at least one button still buttoned is not going to help much. Eliminating clothing with buttons and keeping the neckline high and the blouse tucked in along with a "no-touch" agreement will be much more helpful. Being specific and radical with new starting points is important.

Contributing factors and situations that offer the temptation to compromise should be identified. Late evenings that linger too long, being alone in an apartment or room, work or school pressures, general tiredness and goodbys that take more than five minutes are common culprits. Another one is being "too tired to drive home." Taking specific steps to avoid these situations is important. Some couples have set a timer on a watch or microwave to limit goodbys. Too tired? Take a taxi or call a friend. Having close—geographically as well as emotionally—friends willing to keep you accountable and honest can be a great help.

So what if sexual intimacy boundaries have been crossed—once, a few times or often? It *is* possible to back up, start over and go more slowly. Get help in setting a radical new starting point that redefines the relationship boundaries clearly. Identify tempting situations, attitudes and attire. And remember to evaluate other contributing factors: *time, talk and touch!* Avoiding emotional fornication can greatly help in resisting physical fornication. Establish an accountability resource with a counselor, friend, parent or pastor to encourage your efforts and obedience. This should be a person who exercises both truth and grace in the repentance and restoration process.

And together set some specific rules of conduct. Care for one another enough to let the person who is weaker in a certain area set the limits for conduct accordingly. One couple I knew had to eliminate nearly all movies from their date night because the man had an intense interest in pornography dating from his childhood. Often even a nonexplicit sex scene would trigger memories and images he was working hard to forget. The woman in the relationship was willing to give up movies to gain a godly man. As Christian sisters and brothers in God's kingdom we are called to "do nothing out of selfish ambition or vain conceit, but in humility consider others better than yourselves" (Philippians 2:3).

Obedience to this command would, of course, solve most fornication problems to begin with, but it is never too late to learn. The later the lesson begins, the harder it may be to learn. But our God is an awesome God. He feeds multitudes with loaves and fishes, speaks to reluctant disciples through burning bushes, parts the sea and walks on water. The "what ifs" of life are opportunities for God to show us the fullness of his grace and truth. That's when we will see his glory in Jesus, who loves us no matter what.

We can be confident in Jesus. He understands our weakness because he has shared our life, but not our sin, as a human being. He does not excuse or condone our weakness, because he is the sinless Son of a holy Father. Because this is true, we can believe the Scriptures that tell us that "the Word became flesh and lived among us" and that in Jesus Christ we see God's glory, "the glory as of a father's only son, *full of grace and truth.*" And from this fullness "we have all received, grace upon grace" (John 1:14, 16 NRSV) to back up, start over, go slowly and get it right.

10

Autoerotic Activity & the Sisters at ΔΘΣ

THERE ARE NO ROCKS in my pockets." This is one of my favorite expressions of what it means to be forgiven. For those who come to get some advice, or to confess some sin, this expression is my way of saying, "People who know they are forgiven have no room to condemn others." No matter how great the trouble or how deep the sense of shame, the cross of Jesus is greater and deeper. There is no sin, short of refusing the cross, that cannot be redeemed by the work of God in Jesus Christ. The story of Jesus' forgiving the woman caught in sexual sin in the eighth chapter of John's Gospel is a story for every person who desires to "go and sin no more." There is no sinful person beyond the boundaries of God's judgment—nor beyond his mercy and grace.

Faithfulness Greater Than Failure
Regrets, however, still exist in the light of redemption. To be

forgiven includes the merciful forgetfulness of God ("I . . . will remember their sins no more," Jeremiah 31:34), but our memories are not so quickly cleansed. This is not altogether bad; when we couple our memories with a greater sense of grace, remembering our sin can help us walk more wisely on the road of obedience and faith. But when memories of sin overwhelm our sense of God's grace, our walk with the Lord is so burdensome that we grow weary and can cease to function as disciples doing the work of the kingdom.

In the third chapter of Philippians, Paul "remembers" his sin-filled and futile life before he encountered the risen Christ (vv. 4-7). He ends this rehearsal of regret by stating his desires for maturity in the Christian life (vv. 8-12). Then Paul writes, "One thing I do: *Forgetting* what is behind and straining toward what is ahead, I *press on* toward the goal to win the prize for which God has called me heavenward in Christ Jesus" (vv. 13-14). Paul's "forgetting" did not erase his memory, but his sin-filled past was not the influence that determined his obedience in living out the life of a Christian.

What did Paul have to forget? Nothing less than a murderous rampage against the infant church. As a young man, Paul watched while Stephen, an outspoken believer in Christ, was stoned to death. Paul went on to root out followers of Christ, taking them from their homes and imprisoning them (Acts 7:58-60; 8:3; Galatians 1:13-14). These are not images easily erased. Paul *remembered* he had been a persecutor, and this fueled his zeal for evangelism and the purity of the gospel's truth. Yet Paul also *forgot* these things in the light of God's grace and the work of Christ that makes all things new (2 Corinthians 5:17). Paul *pressed on* to a future that was filled with hope because he had a Savior who loved him in spite of his past. Paul had regrets, but he also had a Redeemer. Paul knew the truest love in a world of false hopes.

The verb translated to "press on" (vv. 12 and 14) is the Greek word *diōkō*. It was a word associated with hunting or participating in a footrace. It carries with it the sense of putting forth a maximum effort in reaching a goal. Every muscle is taut with the exertion demanded of the endeavor that is undertaken. Paul couldn't afford to invest energy over the past, regretting mistakes he could not undo. He recognized there are no "do-overs" in real life; there are no outtakes that don't show up in the final product. In the middle of a live performance, he refused to run off stage. Paul pressed on with a faithfulness that would grow greater than his failure.

Many people have profound regrets over past sexual conduct. Sexual sin can happen before conversion to Christ, but sexual sin can also happen well after spiritual rebirth. In either scenario, sexual memories are not easily erased from our minds. Not only is this true because sex is such a powerful human appetite, but also because the adversary, Satan, works in the spiritual realm to keep unholy imprints in our minds to accuse our hearts. Who can deny that curse words or advertising jingles are easier to memorize than Scripture? Many remember the hard-to-get-out-of-your-head pornographic pictures in some magazine, but can't recall an illustration in a textbook that they have studied!

Like Paul, however, Christians are not to use regretful memories as a defining influence in our lives. If Paul had dwelt on his past life, he may have been immobilized in his ministry and disobedient to the call of God. To be obediently responsive to God's greater claim on his life, Paul had to choose to "forget" the past and "press on" to a future where mercies are new every morning. God's faithfulness is always greater than our sin, and his steadfast love is the reason for our hope (Lamentations 3:22-24). Sexual sin may cause painful and persistent regret, but it is one paradox of salvation that disciples can *remember and forget* at the same time. Past sin can make us wiser, but in Christ there is "no condemnation" (Romans 8:1).

Evan and Erica

During the early years of our ministry, my husband counseled a young man who was growing increasingly serious in his relationship with a woman. They were both active members of our church. Evan had surrendered his life to Christ in the later years of high school, and Erica had come to Christ at a very early age. Erica had dated a little, but she was a virgin. Evan had "lost" his virginity during his freshman year in high school. It had been a one-time thing, uncomfortable in a car, and highly dissatisfying. All these things, coupled with nearly being found out by a nosy dog and its owner, were enough to keep Evan physically chaste until the day he came to talk to Breck.

Evan wanted to know how to tell Erica about this lustful liaison years in the past. He was pretty sure that to tell Erica was the right thing to do. He had a sense that the weight of a secret would be heavier than any confession of sin. Breck reassured Evan that this was very true. If Erica loved Evan and truly accepted the forgiveness of God, she would forgive her brother in Christ and accept Evan as her husband. Breck's advice was to pray for Erica's heart to be prepared for this confession, for Evan's confession to be clearly penitent and for their relationship to continue to grow in honesty and love.

Evan and Breck prayed together, and a short while later, Evan told Erica about his past sexual experience. Erica was disappointed but not entirely surprised. Evan had told her about some excessive drinking and partying prior to his conversion. Erica had wondered but didn't know how or if to ask Evan about his past sexual conduct. As they grew more in love and their commitment to each other was enriched by a Christ-centered attitude of acceptance and grace, Erica had decided that the status of Evan's virginity no longer carried much importance with her.

Still, knowing for sure was a bit unsettling, and it took Erica a little while to relax completely with Evan's physical affection toward her. Both Evan and Erica openly acknowledged this brief time of assimilation and adjustment. They were prayerful with and for each other and patient with each other's feelings.

Erica and Evan were married, went off to seminary and eventually into full-time ministry. Years later we heard the news that a baby was on the way. This was especially wonderful because getting pregnant had been difficult for them. Breck and I also knew what a healing event this would be for Evan. You see, years after he and Erica were married and had begun to purposefully try to conceive a child, Evan had come to talk to Breck and me. He began by saying, "Theologically I know that what I feel is really impossible, but I need to talk it out, and you two are the only ones that know my whole story."

For years Evan hadn't given one thought to his past life, but when Erica failed to conceive, a question entered his mind: what if this is punishment for my sexual impurity? Evan assured us that he knew what he would say to others who came to him with the same concern. He would talk about forgiveness and grace and Romans 8:1 and 2 Corinthians 5:17, about God's love and mercy and the need to forgive yourself. He knew what he believed, but he just felt guilty and regretful.

We cried with Evan, counseled him as he would others, and prayed with him to know the love and grace and goodness of God in a deeper way than ever before. And we prayed that the work of the cross would completely bear away the final emotional scars of Evan's past.

When Evan left that day, Breck and I were struck again by the persistent memory of sexual conduct. The emotional baggage of a one-night transgression had burdened our brother in Christ for a decade and a half! For more than ninety-nine percent of the time, it was the farthest thing from Evan's mind, but at an opportune moment of self-doubt, condemnation found its mark in Evan's heart. Breck and I were confident that Evan would be able, by God's immeasurable grace, to *forget* what was behind and *press on* to a future purposed by God.

He did. And their names are Kristie, Karrie, Karl and Kevin. To this day Evan and Erica serve the Lord as a family of faith. Evan and Erica learned to speak the truth in love, extend the forgiveness given to them in Christ, and accept the same forgiveness for themselves. Evan and Erica have embraced the freedom and fullness of what it means to *forget* and *press on*. This exercise of faith is never easy, but for some it is more pain-filled than it was for Erica and Evan.

Brett and Anna

Before coming to Christ in her college years, Anna had been sexually very active. Her roommate during her junior year was a Christian who prayerfully and carefully led Anna to Christ and brought her to our church for worship, discipleship and counseling. It was a joy to see Anna "love much," knowing she was "forgiven much" (Luke 7:47). She loved Bible study and never could get enough. About a year after her rebirth Anna met a young man at work who also knew the Lord, and they began a good friendship. During the course of the friendship, a romance developed. By this time Breck and I knew Anna and Brett pretty well. Both were active in our church and in a Bible study at the office where they were employed.

Within the first few weeks of dating, Anna told Brett about her promiscuous past. Previously she had told him about her unhappy childhood and teenage drinking, but she had not mentioned her sexual lifestyle before coming to Christ. At the time Brett reassured Anna that he understood and accepted this as a part of her past. So the romance continued, and the sense of commitment began to grow in each of them. By this time both Anna and Brett had graduated from college, and they seriously considered marriage as a sooner-than-later possibility.

Brett called one day and asked if he could come over to talk to me. He sounded very tense on the phone, and when he arrived I could tell he had been crying and was visibly very distraught. Brett began the conversation with these words: "Robbie, I know what I believe. I know what I should feel and be able to do, but I can't. I just can't." Brett went on to tell me how Anna's past was keeping him from being able to make a lifelong commitment to her. He felt he could not marry her. "I just can't get images out of my mind. I know this is wrong. I know God has forgiven Anna. I even forgive Anna—theologically. Emotionally, I can't get past this. I want to love Anna, but at the same time I can't love Anna."

Brett had been raised in the Christian faith, in a functional family with values well taught and well modeled. He was a virgin, and all his life had assumed he would marry a virgin. Anna's past was a disappointment that Brett couldn't get over. His pain came from the dissonance he felt between his theology of forgiveness and grace and his emotional inability to apply this to Anna. It became so painful that Brett felt he could no longer continue in the relationship.

The evening before Brett came to see me, he had talked to Anna, telling her what he felt and how wrong he felt for feeling this way, and that he thought it best for them to end the relationship. Brett was in agony over who he was, who Anna had been and how he could ever sort out his theological beliefs and his human feelings. Anna had been heartbroken at Brett's decision, but she recognized the depth of his pain and felt worse for him! She had encouraged him to talk it all out with someone, and this was why he had called.

So Brett talked, and I listened. He cried, and I prayed. Brett knew the *truth* about his situation, but he needed to know the *grace.* Somehow he wanted to learn grace like he had learned the truth. He wanted to feel the right, compassionate and theologically correct things. From the first time Anna told Brett about her past and up until the evening before our meeting,

Brett had tried saying the right, compassionate and theolog-ically correct things. He had hoped that this exercise of "faith" would make his feelings follow obediently. It had worked in other situations, but not now. So Brett asked me, "What's wrong? Why can't I get over this? When will I be able to truly forgive?"

I answered gently, "Brett, most people learn to truly forgive when they experience the real depth of needing forgiveness themselves." Brett was a sinner, but he was a "good guy" too. His sinful nature hadn't lent itself to much overt rebellion. Brett's trouble with forgiveness stemmed partly from his own lack of the *experience* of forgiveness. He embraced by faith the fact of forgiveness and the necessary work of Christ on the cross. I knew that deepening his experience in grace of the facts of the gospel's truth was something only God could do. This is completely the work of the Spirit. He alone can bring conviction without condemnation.

I shared this with Brett, and we ended our time with prayer. My answer that day proved to be the truth several years later. He wrote me a letter from grad school telling me about a foolish and sinful decision he made. It didn't have anything to do with his sexual conduct, but it was wrong and professionally costly. He closed the letter writing, "It was hard for me to realize I could ever do anything so wrong and stupid and sinful. This was a tough and humbling lesson. But you were right about this: I sure am a lot more forgiving now that I am the desperate object of needing the forgiveness of others. Remem-bering what you said has helped me get through this."

For me a special symbol of the hope, forgiveness and grace of God is that fact that both Anna and Brett married other Christians and have established wonderful homes. Anna's sense of forgetting and pressing on kept her from feeling shame or accepting condemnation during the time her rela-tionship with Brett ended. Her experience of profound forgiveness kept her from resenting Brett during the time of this heartbreak. She is married to a godly man who fully loves and accepts her. Brett also married a godly woman who loves and accepts him for who he is.

Some lessons in faith and love are painful. But God is faithful, and he is true to his promise that "he who began a good work in [us] will carry it on to completion" (Philippians 1:6). God will finish his work in our lives. Like his Son, he wants us to be his children "full of grace and truth." As a good Father, he understands how difficult it can be for us to learn how to be full of both, and he will give us time to learn. God's hardest lessons always begin in grace and end in mercy, but in between we find out we have more to learn than we ever thought.

Roger

Through the years more than a few men like Roger have come to talk to my husband or me. The problem? Questions, doubts, anxiety about masturbation. Many times this is the last thing a person considers when sexual release is sought through self-stimulation. Masturbation is a habit that is usually formed during periods of loneliness and ends up being hidden by withdrawal and isolation. This autoerotic activity, in both men and women, is one way that feelings of loneliness actually can be intensified. Masturbation generally only worsens the problem it attempts to address.

In addition, masturbation often fosters increasingly erotic fantasies. This can be significantly detrimental to experiencing a satisfying sexual life with one's spouse. Whether a person is presently married or anticipating marriage in the future, masturbation fantasies can create unrealistic expectations for sexual experience. In this way autoeroticism is a form of unfaithfulness. Masturbation seeks to satisfy but leads to increasing dissatisfaction.

When Christian men and women who want to mature in

their relationship with God begin to struggle with this problem, they often want to approach it like any other problem. "Just don't," they tell themselves. "Stay busy" can seem like a good solution. "Tell no one and pray" sounds like safe advice. Or "tell everyone, and pray about it constantly" will create accountability. Now there may be a kernel of wisdom in much of this instinctive self-counsel, but all these basic ideas tend to make either too much or too little of this fleshly self-indulgence.

Masturbation can be a habit that feels as addictive as any drug. The body can begin to feel like the anticipated release is necessary. Christians realize that any bodily habit can create a bondage to the self that denies the Holy Spirit control of one's life. Ephesians 5:18 admonishes the children of God, "Do not get drunk on wine, which leads to debauchery. Instead, be filled with the Spirit." Anything that compromises influence or denies control of the Holy Spirit in our lives is not faith. Christians are called to "live by faith, not by sight" (2 Corinthians 5:7). In fact, the verses that precede the prohibition of drunkenness quoted above are, "Be very careful, then, how you live—not as unwise but as wise, making the most of every opportunity, because the days are evil. Therefore do not be foolish, but understand what the Lord's will is" (Ephesians 5:15-17).

The Scripture makes it clear that one good way to combat what is foolish and wasteful is to understand the will of God. Doing what is good is often the best way to avoid what is not helpful and not wise. While staying busy may be basically sound advice, what a person *does* to "stay busy" may be more important to consider. Concentrating on the problem, talking about it to many others, constantly focusing on the struggle in prayer and memorizing Bible verses about temptation may, in fact, be counterproductive.

Roger and many others through the years have found an approach that positively focuses on the will of God to be very helpful. I recommend one, maybe two, accountability partners—trusted people who can pray with you or get with you when the going gets tough. This is important no matter what the struggle. Roger ended up talking to the youth pastor of his church who was more than willing to hold him accountable.

It is good to identify other habits or situations that are physically or emotionally linked with the urge to masturbate. Of course there is no place for any kind of pornography in a Christian's life, but other movies, magazines and music may have to be eliminated as well. In disconnecting the habit from familiar routines, the latter often have to be disrupted. Move furniture, eat at a different time, get a new bedspread and begin new times to wake in the morning and go to bed at night. Since the bathroom was Roger's greatest place of temptation, he moved most of his toiletries elsewhere to minimize his time there. He also moved his furniture and traded bedrooms with his housemate.

Try to shift your focus from "inward" to "outward." Begin some new and different part of serving others in a ministry that is completely remote from the problem. In other words, volunteering to disciple a younger Christian in the area of sexual temptation may not be the best way to deal with your own problems at the same time. A better idea may be to help collect canned goods and clothing for migrant farmers. Roger volunteered to do all the lawn care for the local crisis pregnancy counseling center.

Scripture study and memorization can be invaluable during this time of learning a new dimension of self-control. Be aware however that concentrating on verses about resisting temptation, avoiding sin or establishing self-control can make things more difficult. It's like telling yourself over and over again, "Don't think of a purple monkey." All you can think of is a purple monkey. The idea is to learn what the will of God is, to concentrate on the positive—what is right, not the negative that you hope to overcome.

A good way of focusing on the positive is studying and memorizing Scripture that has to do with praise and thanksgiving. Roger memorized several psalms and nearly the entire book of Philippians. I might add that he memorized the last part of Philippians out of a new and satisfying habit of the heart, not as an attempt to break a habit of the flesh.

These basic ideas can be used to resist any temptation to self-indulgence. Good counseling, good work, good thoughts and good Scripture can be used of God to escape a bad habit. The sad thing about masturbation is that it just doesn't do any good. It's a waste. Nocturnal emissions and climactic dreams are physical ways humans can deal with the tension experienced by sexually adult bodies. Literally "taking things into your own hands" is a lack of faith in the Creator to provide "a way out so that [we] can stand up under" temptation (1 Corinthians 10:13).

Henry

"Pornography is invisible assault and battery on people made in the image of God." This quote from my husband makes more than a few people sit up and listen. Like the fantasies often associated with masturbation, pornography creates isolation and loneliness, and it is visual infidelity. Unlike masturbation, another person is involved. The people on the page or screen belong to families. They are someone's son or daughter. They are people created in God's image and far from home.

Pornography offers opportunities for the lust that Jesus equates with adultery (Matthew 5:28). Jesus recognizes the ultimately lethal nature of sin when he insists his disciples deal radically with temptation and anything that offends the image of God in the human person. Matthew 5:29-30 states that the radical denial of the "eye" or "hand" is a way to preserve the body for a life of righteousness. With pornography radical rejection is vital. In a positive sense Jesus says, "Whatever is true, whatever is noble, whatever is right, whatever is pure, whatever is lovely, whatever is admirable . . . think about such things" (Philippians 4:8). Pornography denies to the core all of those attributes and has no place in the mind and heart guarded by Christ Jesus (Philippians 4:7).

Henry had been raised in a home where pornography was openly accepted. His dad subscribed to a popular adult magazine, and as Henry grew older he was aware that his parents watched pornographic movies. They subscribed to the adult cable-TV channel, and although it was "off-limits" to the kids in the family, Henry and his brother watched it regularly when their parents were not at home.

Pornographic images greatly influenced Henry's expectations for sex, and when he had intercourse for the first time it was less thrilling than he had assumed it would be. Henry became more sexually active, looking for the thrill, and finally tried some homoerotic activity that proved painful and dissatisfying. Henry went off to college certain about his sexual identity but wondering if porn was the only way to capture the thrill.

During his first semesters, Henry's dorm room was known as "Centerfold Central." Posters, magazines and VCR tapes were common vehicles for recreational lust for many young men on his hall and for some of their girlfriends. Henry, however, didn't have a girlfriend. He had a video collection and a string of one-night sexual episodes.

I learned about Henry's past after his conversion to Christ during his sophomore year. Henry had attended a campus evangelistic event, heard the gospel, and believed it. He got to know some of the students involved in planning the event, began to attend their small-group Bible study and grow in his newfound faith. I had no idea of Henry's background when I met him a few months later and he asked to talk to me about "a problem."

Henry felt trapped by his life with pornography. The more he got to know Jesus and met Christians who had not had his experience with pornography, the more he felt helpless to be a "first-class" Christian. In the first wave of his postconversion life, he had gotten rid of his magazines and tapes. But he now found that he was constantly tempted at newsstands and video stores. He masturbated regularly and indulged in erotic fantasies. He wanted to be different, yet didn't have any idea where to start.

Although Henry never followed through on establishing an accountability partner, he tried nearly everything I suggested. Once. He rearranged his dorm room—but kept his favorite poster rolled up on the top shelf of his closet. He memorized two verses and then said, "It doesn't work for me." Henry felt he had to study on small-group Bible study night. Slowly he returned to old friends who shared magazines and tapes. He excused these associations with "I don't own them, and I can't help it if people I'm around have them." Henry felt repentant at times, but he was never willing to be radically repentant.

Henry eventually transferred to another school and moved in with a former girlfriend, and now says he "tried Christianity once." Henry's response to God had been like all the unreceptive kinds of soil on which the seed of the Word was sown in Jesus' parable (Mark 4:1-20). The worldliness of pornography choked out the seed. The rocky soil of his soul provided no depth for roots to grow deeply, and Henry was unwilling to do the hard work of moving rocks. Like the birds in Jesus' parable, the accuser plucked the Word from Henry's hardened heart.

Henry's story has yet to have an element of hope or godly direction. How God works in the life of another contains mystery, in some more than others it seems. The friends who witnessed to Henry are not responsible for his salvation. We are responsible to continue telling the truth and exercising grace at every opportunity Henry will allow and every opening we can faithfully initiate. By telling Henry's story, I do not want to suggest that exposure to pornography can create a hopeless situation. I do want to bring a sobering attitude to the power of sin in images designed to create lust.

Much of Henry's early exposure to pornography was unsought by Henry and uncensored by his parents. In this sense, Henry had a harder row to hoe that others seeking victory over this fleshly self-indulgence. But many times exposure to pornography begins in locker rooms, bedroom closets and parties around a VCR, when those involved are at an age of personal accountability. Nothing short of complete refusal to entertain any sort of pornography will lead to godliness. If what you see offends God or causes you to sin, cut yourself completely out of the situation. If what you desire to touch offends God or causes you to sin, pluck yourself out of touching distance immediately. Pornography is not going to go away. It's the Christian who has to repent radically and get away. This is the gist of the stern admonition and command of Jesus recorded in Matthew 5:29-30.

Grace and Truth

Grace and Truth are twin sisters living over at Delta Theta Sigma. The thirty-seconds-older sister, Grace, always makes sure people know they are loved by God no matter what. She reminds people that no sin is so great that the work of Jesus on the cross of Calvary is not greater. Her sister, Truth, makes sure people know that God is always holy no matter what. She reminds people that it cost God the life of his only begotten Son to deal radically with our sin. Grace listens well, and Truth speaks clearly. Grace provides the energy needed to forget the past and press on to the future. Truth provides the picture of what that future is supposed to look like.

Grace and Truth. Jesus knew them fully and well. And when "the Word became flesh," that's when we beheld "his glory, the glory of the One and Only, who came from the Father" (John

1:14). When the Word takes up residence in our heart and fills us with both grace and truth, our created flesh has the possibility to reflect the glory won for us in God's Son.

Grace meets us where we are. Truth reminds us of how far we have to go. Grace assures our hearts that we will make it. Truth tells us how. Grace and truth need to be our companions on the journey to sexual purity and a life of holiness as we edge toward Eden.

11

Sinful Saints

RECLAIMING GOD'S DESIRE for sexual relationships has never been easy. Finding true love in the middle of a world of false hopes and few expectations can seem far-fetched. When parents fail in marriages or relationships, their children can say, "Why bother even to try finding a love that lasts?" When leaders of God's people yield to sexual sin and destroy their personal credibility as well as their ministries, the last hope for helpful role models seemingly evaporates.

It's certainly not just a recent phenomenon that some in God's service have disobeyed his will in the area of sexual conduct. In the age of mass media, however, celebrities are created and exposed by publicity. *Everyone* hears about compromises of conduct. The knowledge of sin is no longer confined to those immediately affected by the behavior. Church leaders, teachers and pastors are in special need of prayer. Holiness—obedience to God's will and heart—matters.

Two major factors contribute to the sexual sin of those in

leadership. One is the lack of accountability to others for pastoral direction and spiritual care. The leader ends up trying to take care of himself or herself, and corrective counsel can be lost. It is unwise to live a life of increasing independence no matter who you are, what your leadership role is or how many other people depend on you. If you are a fool to hire yourself as your own lawyer, you are a fraud to have yourself as your own counselor.

The second major factor contributing to sexual sin by those in leadership is Satan, who knows that leaders can bring others down with them in their sin. First Peter 5:8 describes this ravenous agenda: "Your enemy the devil prowls around like a roaring lion looking for someone to devour." Peter's advice to "be self-controlled and alert. . . . Resist him, standing firm in the faith" is for all God's people, but leaders need to recognize a more intentional enemy.

Those in leadership need to acknowledge that they are especially tasty targets for this evil lion because of how an entire ministry can be maligned and eventually destroyed. Whether heads of a nation or heads of families, people others look up to are those the devil delights to see fall from such height. Jesson and Babbs were two people who had a sexual one-nighter. It didn't end up on the pages of the supermarket tabloids, but people in our church still talk about it years after.

Jesson and Babbs

Jesson, the CEO of a successful enterprise, was nearing middle age. In the early years he had to travel a lot. He was ambitious and talented; he had the knack of gathering teams of bright entrepreneurs and making a dime into a dollar. He married, had children, but home life was rarely given the same attention of that given a new product or campaign. Jesson did have an earnest love for God. He rarely missed worship, even when on the road. He particularly liked hymns, and, as much as he was a go-getter, he also kept a journal and prayed regularly. Jesson's relationship with God was serious, and seemed to thrive in times of crisis.

Jesson had learned some painful lessons along the way to success, and he was now getting tired of running the show, traveling and the rat race in general. He wanted to clear his calendar, stay home and be near his family, and work on projects closer to his corporate headquarters. So he took some extended time off, going in to the office a few times a week for a few hours. He wanted to learn to relax.

Things went well at first. Jesson had able partners in his company who were competent and trustworthy. His business continued to grow, and although some situations lacked the charisma that Jesson brought to meetings and strategy, he resisted the pleas of others to return to work full time.

After some time Jesson found that he was increasingly bored. He wondered if he might be depressed since he slept a lot and had little appetite, but he resisted going to a counselor or confiding in his pastor or a close friend. It may have just been hard for him to shift the pace of a lifetime. He was made for on-site leadership and the challenges of conquering something new and exciting.

His boredom increased, and Jesson ended up having a one-night affair with a beautiful woman who caught his eye. She lived nearby in the same swank subdivision. Even though Jesson didn't know her well at all, they found themselves together after a party and it "just happened." It was only a one-night stand, and no one else was home. Jesson didn't tell anyone, but he did talk to himself. *Who did it hurt? No one will know. I'm not the first man to have an affair. More people would be hurt if it became known. What would my pastor think? And I'm an elder in the church! No, I'll just keep quiet, and I won't see Babbs again.*

It Gets Worse

Jesson's personal sin and guilt became a greater problem when he discovered that Babbs was a married woman. To make matters completely unavoidable, Babbs had become pregnant. This all happened before abortion was legal in this country, and besides, as a believer, Jesson considered abortion to be murder. Babbs never considered abortion an option in any case.

Babbs's situation was heartbreaking. Her husband, Yuri, was in the military and had been on assignment in the Middle East. This political hotbed was in turmoil, and violence often erupted near where he was stationed. Furloughs home were few and far between for Babbs's husband, and there was no way the baby could be his. Babbs had been flattered by this wealthy and well-known man's attention, and in the middle of her loneliness, went along with his advances. But now she was alone with her problem. She had no reason to believe her family or her husband's would stand by her at this time, since she and Yuri had married each other against the wishes of both their families.

Babbs was desperate and went to Jesson in a panic. She didn't care about his career, public reputation, family concerns or his standing in the church—she just needed some kind of help.

At first Jesson treated this news just like any stroke of bad luck in a company deal. He called in experts to see what could be done. He didn't tell anyone what was really going on, but he knew how to get the information he wanted. The simplest thing was to get her husband out of the Middle East, home on furlough so that he would have relations with Babbs. Jesson had no intention of marrying Babbs even if that had been an option. Jesson made a few calls to friends with clout in the military, and in about two weeks, Babbs's husband was sent home.

But there was a problem: the couple did not make love. Yuri

was preoccupied by the situation he had left. The many hard-ships and traumatic events in the military confrontation had deeply affected him. He came home emotionally depleted, guilt-ridden by leaving his responsibilities, and he couldn't bring himself to feign any kind of affection for his wife. It was a turbulent and sad situation. The more Babbs tried to communicate and get close to Yuri, the more he resisted her and resented her advances. Jesson had suggested that Babbs try to loosen up and party some with her husband, but even with excessive drinking, sexual relations did not occur. Babbs was distraught, Jesson was fed up with the whole thing, and Yuri said he just wanted to get back to his outfit.

Worse Yet
Pulling some more strings with Pentagon-types, Jesson maneuvered to get Yuri assigned to a particularly vulnerable assignment near the guerrilla fighting taking place. With Yuri out of the way, he could work things out eventually to marry Babbs, and no one would be the wiser. Jesson's self-protective instincts were so strong that all he could think of was keeping this secret. He was willing to hurt his family, marry a wife he did not love and actually allow a man to be killed to facilitate the whole charade.

Sadly, Jesson's plan succeeded. Yuri was killed. Jesson divorced his wife and married Babbs, alienating his family in the process. His new young wife was tense and fairly unhappy. She had all she ever wanted materially, but the pregnancy was a constant reminder of what they had done. After the child was born, Babbs gave the baby all her attention. Jesson tried to bury his guilt by paying attention to this child as he had none of his other children. During all this, Jesson felt completely estranged in his relationship with God.

A year passed, and Jesson just went through the motions of life. His company did well, but his division managers didn't trust him as they once did. Jesson was not himself, and it was obvious something was very wrong. No one knew how to help him.

His pastor, an acquaintance of my husband, finally went to Jesson to get to the bottom of things. Jesson was expecting something like a business meeting about the progress on the new worship sanctuary; he had donated a substantial sum and had secured an architect, and the pastor kept him informed about how things were going. But this was a pastoral call, not a business meeting.

Through prayer, thought and the Spirit's discernment, the pastor confronted Jesson with what he thought was the problem. "Jesson, you had everything a man could ever want, and it wasn't enough. You had to have an affair. You got caught, ruthlessly covered your tracks, and now can't live with yourself. I'm right, aren't I, Jesson? You are the man I just described."

Jesson's face turned pale. His gaze dropped to his feet. His hands grew clammy, and his shoulders sagged. He was caught. Pastor Nate had figured it out. How many others knew? It didn't matter now. God knew.

And Jesson looked up with tear-filled eyes and with a shaking voice said simply, "I have sinned against the Lord." This, of course, was the *truth*. But with equal *grace* his pastor replied, "The Lord has also taken away your sin."

An Old Story with Renewed Meaning

Babbs and Jesson's story, of course, is found in 2 Samuel 11—12. It is an unvarnished account of Bathsheba, the wife of Uriah the Hittite, and God's finest hymnwriter and greatest king—David, son of Jesse. Long before this sinful episode, David was called "a man after [God's] own heart" (1 Samuel 13:14). What is startling is that centuries later, in Acts 13:22, David's life is remembered with the same epitaph! How can it be that David is known as a man after God's heart when he was guilty of adultery, murder, manipulation, hypocrisy, fraudulence and a pride so self-protective that he would actually sacrifice his own family and kingdom to hide his sin?

Talk about sexual regret! I doubt if any person ever to read this book could be labeled with David's litany of sin. How could a person with a history of such sexual sin be restored to a rich and right relationship to God? "Pastor Nate," or Nathan, said it well, "The LORD has taken away your sin. You are not going to die." So who did die for David's sin? The Lord Jesus Christ, who takes away the sin of the world. By faith in the work of God *to be done* in his behalf, David believed. In the same way, by faith in the work of God *done* in our behalf, we believe. To reassure us of the completeness and final reality of our forgiveness, God raised Jesus from the dead. Believers are not just forgiven, we are given new life in God's Spirit.

But what reassurance did David receive that his sin was forgiven? In our instincts as a lesser god, we probably would have made David impotent and Bathsheba barren, and had the kingdom overtaken by Uriah's relatives, the Hittites! The truth does remain that the child of their sinful liaison became ill and died, and violence and rebellion marked many of David's other children for the rest of his life. The consequences of sin are painful and not easily overturned. But forgiveness is not measured by consequence but by repentance.

God's forgiveness was confirmed for David and Bathsheba in the birth of another child. And not just any child. The second child of David and Bathsheba would become the next king of Israel, Solomon. Now that is grace!

This grace was not cheapened by a casual attitude reflected in a superficial confession. David's sorrow over his sin was deep and life-changing. His repentance came after a sense of alienation from God that made him despair of life itself. In Psalm 51, David's heartbreak is written for all God's people to see. In this psalm David declares that God does not despise a "broken and contrite heart." And after repentance, forgiveness is given by the unmerited grace of God. In David's story this is most clearly seen by the Lord's naming of the infant Solomon. Second Samuel 12:25 states, "because the LORD loved him, he sent word through Nathan the prophet to name him Jedidiah." In Hebrew, Jedidiah means "beloved of the LORD."

What must David and Bathsheba have felt as Nathan took this infant in his arms? Longing for righteousness, and the full portion of forgiveness, what were their hopes and fears? This relationship had started off with nothing but sin, lust, compromise, disobedience and selfishness. Their adulterous union had led to murder, death, sorrow, severe family dysfunction and the starvation of spiritual life. Is redemption really possible for such people? How could anything good and lovely come from their relationship?

With God, nothing is impossible. Here is Jedidiah, the beloved of the Lord. Here is Solomon, the next king of Israel. Here is the truth of repentance and the grace of forgiveness. We too need to know that whatever the sin, sorrow, mess, foul-up or stupidity, whether invited, encouraged, sudden, once or long-term, whether we are the victim or the victimizer, when the sorrow of a broken heart leads to life-changing repentance, God offers us forgiveness and restoration. Yes, we have sinned against God. And, yes, the Lord has taken away our sin. No matter what!

Our Redeemer can take the worst things we want to hide about our lives, and when offered by the confession of a contrite and broken heart, God returns to us a "Jedidiah." Blessing in the place of banishment. Grace in place of grief. Mercy in place of misery. We are the "beloved of the Lord."

Sexual Sin and Forgiveness

This incredible abundance of grace should work in the believer's heart a desire for joyful obedience that outruns all compromise. No matter what our sin, tabloid or trivial, we are called to repentance and a life of holiness. Grace, when received by faith, will not be abused. An appreciation for grace gives us the energy for obedience. The Scripture assures us that the joy of the Lord is our strength (Nehemiah 8:10). That joy is born in the womb of repentance.

It's important to remember that sexual sin is not without consequence. In some sense, sexual sin is more grievous to us than some other acts of disobedience. First Corinthians 6:13-18 warns believers,

> The body is not meant for sexual immorality, but for the Lord. . . . Do you not know that your bodies are members of Christ himself? Shall I then take the members of Christ and unite them with a prostitute? Never! Do you not know that he who unites himself with a prostitute is one with her in body? . . . Flee from sexual immorality. All other sins a man commits are outside his body, but he who sins sexually sins against his own body.

After this clear prohibition Scripture states that our body is in fact a "temple of the Holy Spirit," and we are not the owners of our own body. God's people are bought with the price of Christ's death on the cross, so we can glorify God with our body.

Even in light of the particular ramifications of sexual sin, the potential for restoration and forgiveness is not the only offer. The repentant sinner is promised the capacity to end up actually giving God glory! Sin *will* exact a price from us. But God has paid the higher price with the costly blood of his Son, and we are redeemed, bought back—forgiven and freed to "go and sin no more."

Hope and Healing

When students, friends or parishioners come to me to confess sexual sin, I don't flinch. Usually these people come in the middle of struggling with sorrow, guilt, pain and regret. They are willing to repent but are often unsure if real and complete repentance is possible. This uncertainty comes from a fear that forgiveness is not complete or really possible.

I remember one young man who came to confess some homoerotic fantasy and activity. He began by saying, "Robbie, you will probably just want to get up and leave—maybe even want to throw up when I tell you who I really am and what I've done." My response? "Well, that I cannot do because God has not walked out on me. He can be grieved and disappointed, but God is not surprised or disgusted. I'm glad you came."

In dealing with sexual fear, regret, sin or confusion, find someone to talk to who will listen with grace and speak the truth. Find a pastor like Nathan, who identified David's sin, helped him deal with its consequences, and eventually blessed the fruit of his repentance with God's love. Do all that you need to do to keep from sin, and be especially alert if you are in a position of leadership or if you teach others.

The devil is jealous of Eden's joy and does not want us to return. Denying God's desire is the devil's delight. The adversary seeks to devour whom he will and rob us of one of God's greatest sources of joy, sexual purity that glorifies the Lord.

12

Sexual Disappointments

RELATIONAL HOMELESSNESS threatens our commitment to godly sexuality. Relational homelessness is a refusal or inability to stay long enough in a relationship to really be known and loved by another. It's like emotional "channel surfing"—going from one thing to the next, never making a commitment to the whole. There are three relationships where this can be manifest: with ourselves, with others and with God. When we experience estrangement in one area, the others are affected as well. We have the feeling that we don't really belong, can't be loved and can't love. So we enter a competition of wills instead of a loving relationship, and we end up lonely, never realizing we are never really alone.

First, being estranged from ourselves is lonely. When we are not true to who we are or when we dislike who we are, we turn to other people and use them to meet our superficial needs. Yet our deepest needs remain unfulfilled. Ambivalence about the God-created goodness of our bodies can make sex an expression of lust, not the culmination of love. Being estranged from ourselves can lead to the confusion of sexual identity, exper-imentation with sexual activity, and the frustration of sexual satisfaction.

Edging our way toward Eden, reclaiming God's desire for our sexuality, also brings us closer to being whole emotionally. The Christian life is a journey of becoming who we really are meant to be.

Second, relational homelessness also causes an estrange-ment from others. We are either too afraid or too eager to find true love. In either case, we are lonely. Deeply trusting another person becomes an impossibility. A commitment to marriage is threatening, not promising. Sexuality is expressed by auto-erotic habits or by flirtatious game-playing to vent frustration, or it is denied altogether.

Edging our way toward Eden means learning to travel to-gether as male and female. We acknowledge our sexuality as part of what makes us brothers and sisters in the Father's family. We repent of self-protective attitudes that lead to iso-lation and autonomy. We risk being known and loved while we risk knowing and loving. The Christian life is always a journey we take together.

Third, relational homelessness is a manifestation of distanc-ing ourselves from God, who knows and loves us best of all. If we don't feel the security of being perfectly loved by God, we are afraid. If we don't know God's design and desire for our sexuality, we are at odds with ourselves and alienated from others. The other sex becomes so opposite that we see them as a threat, not a blessing. Without acknowledging God's in-tended goodness for the sexual relationship within marriage, love is a meet-my-needs noun. Without knowing God in the full grace and truth of his son Jesus, love can never be a wash-your-feet verb. In our fears of self, others and God we continue in a relational homelessness that is lonely for longer than a lifetime.

Edging our way toward Eden means going to a place where the light is always on, your Father is always watching for you and your room is perfectly prepared—just the way it was meant to be. The Christian life is a journey home.

This journey home, however, is not without challenge and risk. C. S. Lewis wrote in his Chronicles of Narnia that Aslan was a "good lion," but he was not "safe." Aslan is the figure that allegorically serves as Jesus the Savior, the Lion of Judah. The God revealed in Jesus Christ is good, but, like Aslan, he is not safe. Our journey home is good, but it is not easy. The Christian life is safe in the ultimate sense, but not without the risks, challenges, dangers and trials that make faith a needed reality for us. People edging toward Eden with hope and obedience can find the journey perilous. People can be deeply hurt and wounded by things they did not expect.

Marty

Marty bounced into my office one day to announce her good news. "God's told me who I am going to marry!" She was grinning broadly, and her eyes danced with delight. She went on to tell me that she had met him the week before at church and that they had been in a small group for prayer at the youth rally that evening. Marty said she couldn't get Rick out of her mind all week, and as she prayed for him God had said, "This is the man you will marry." "Aren't you excited?" Marty asked.

Smiling, I told Marty that I would fully share her hope and excitement if we were to discover that God had indicated the same thing to Rick. Since Marty hadn't talked to Rick about it, she didn't know about that. She reassured me that she would just continue to pray for him and that they would get together in God's time. Until then, she would trust the Lord and be happy.

I promised to pray faithfully that Marty's future be clearly guided and confirmed by the Lord's work. I encouraged Marty by affirming that God does not play "hide and seek" with our feelings or his desire; he delights to confirm his will in our lives. But I also cautioned her that God's will is not unilaterally revealed for any great length of time. If in fact it was God's leading in her prayer time, Rick had been given or would soon be given the same word.

Marty was absolutely confident that this was God's word to her, and she was impatient with my reluctance to automatically agree with her. I reassured her that it *could* be God's word to her and that if it was, the Lord would bring it about. I did suggest that she keep this to herself for a while, waiting for greater discernment and the manifestation of evidence—the fruit of the Spirit's work.

I told Marty about my own experience with a word like this. It wasn't given to me, but to a woman who mentored me in my Christian walk in the early years. Georgia was the wife of the camp director at Big Oak Ranch, where I worked as a nurse the summer I met Breck. After our engagement was announced, Georgia told me, "I'm not surprised. I knew it all along."

Our romance had certainly surprised me, so I asked Georgia when and how she knew. She replied, "It was the first time you came to the office together to ask permission to leave the ranch for an outing. When you walked in, I clearly felt I heard the Lord say, 'Grant their request. This summer is for them.' "

This was news to me! Georgia responded to my incredulous expression by saying, "That's why you and Breck got to go. We had a campfire that night, and usually we keep the ranch nurse around. I told Dodson [her husband] what I felt the Lord had said to me, and we responded in faith."

I asked her why she hadn't said anything at the time. She explained, "If it really was a word from the Lord, he would work it out. I was to watch and pray. And it sure has been fun to see God confirm his word and know that Dodson and I were a part of his will for you."

Georgia had had a very humble response to this situation. The word from the Lord did not contribute any sense of spiritual pride; it evoked only a sense of quiet watchfulness and prayerfulness. She made it clear that one big reason that she didn't share her feeling with me was the possibility that she could have heard wrongly.

Many times, especially in areas of personal desire, it's good to trust God to work out his word while you watch and pray. This allows you time to see if it is God's voice and will, and not your own. Trusting God's Spirit does not eliminate caution about our own sinful tendencies. I saw this in Georgia and learned to watch and pray when I have experienced a "word from the Lord."

I tried to tell Marty about discerning the difference between faith and self-deception. Faith is marked by a humility that continues to seek, trust and hear what God wants to say. Self-deception is marked by an insistence that is spiritually proud and unwilling to admit that "the heart is deceitful above all things" (Jeremiah 17:9). True faith is exercised with humility and an openness to continue to hear God's will. When God speaks, he keeps speaking.

Marty held on to her "promise" for a long time. Rick dated other Christian women in the church but never did ask Marty out. After several years Rick married another Christian woman, and they had three children. Fifteen years later, Marty is still single; she is very lonely and wonders why she held on to her "promise" so tightly. She refused to date others or allow herself to grow close to any other Christian man. I wish I could tell you this was an isolated incident. But it isn't.

Gene
Gene was a young man who received a similar promise, not through prayer but from a conference speaker's "prophecy."

Wanda, the "wife of promise," had gone out with Gene a few times prior to this, but her interest was growing in another relationship. When Gene told her about the prophecy, Wanda was open enough to pray about it, seek counsel from her pastor and give the Lord time to direct her heart. But she never felt at all led to pursue the relationship. Gene resisted the advice of friends in his church to submit this prophecy to his pastor or elders. He ended up going to another church, still insisting that someday Wanda would love him. After several years Wanda fell in love and married a godly man.

Gene is still single and finds it hard to settle down in a church, a job or a friendship. He admits that he may have been wrong to put such confidence in the prophecy, but he continues to think that Wanda was disobedient. In addition to harboring a basic distrust in others, Gene finds it hard to pray in faith and believe that God will guide his future clearly.

We may find it difficult to discern the difference between spiritual pride born of self-deception and godly confidence in a real word from the Lord. Self-deception may occur when we respond too hastily to a word we don't mind hearing. If God has spoken, there is no hurry, no reason to rush, no sense of urgency. God confirms and manifests his promises in time and space. He does this in Scripture, and he does this in our lives. Wait and pray. Watch and pray.

Holding on to a false promise or prophecy as Marty and Gene did is not a frequent problem in my work with students and young people in the church and on campus, but it's not unusual either. Other counselors, youth pastors, campus ministers, students and parents have shared similar stories with me, not just about romance but also about jobs, geographical moves and calls to the mission field or full-time ministry. The longing for certainty may make it easier to accept a "word" without discernment. Reliance on "prophecy" can be used to avoid the uncertainty and risk of dating and courtship.

People like Marty and Gene find it incredibly difficult to refocus their faith after a painful personal disappointment. The exhilaration of believing God to have spoken a special word is only matched by the depth of despair when this word proves to be other than what they assumed. The attitude of *assumption* can be a signal that a genuine word has not been heard and self-deception is in progress.

I always hope that people who come to me have heard the Lord correctly. I want to believe God with them. Having faith in God is central to the Christian life. But when people make assumptions about a future outcome, I urge them to continue to listen and pray for concrete reassurance that they have understood correctly. This will help ensure their future obedience.

True faith is not put off or discouraged by this admonition to listen and pray. True faith trusts God to keep his promises. He knows our frailty, "remembers that we are dust" (Psalm 103:14). He even shared our humanity in Jesus Christ. Through Christ we can approach God with confidence "that we may receive mercy and find grace to help us in our time of need" (Hebrews 4:16). God does not begrudge us his continued help. He knows we need encouragement for our faith to remain steadfast.

Healthy faith is humble faith. People who truly trust God are always hesitant to trust themselves. The heart that recognizes how easily it can be deceived, especially by the promise of good things, is a heart that learns to trust God's goodness fully.

As we struggle to discern the truth of a promise or prophecy, God will strengthen us and give us confirmation: God's true word to us will be confirmed for our faith with evidence. This evidence will generally be more than just the ultimate "answer"; it will involve encouraging progress or signs that lead us to prayer and obedience. This is not just true for romantic concerns, but for vocational wisdom, evangelistic opportunities and other issues of the Christian life. Pray and keep praying. Hear and keep hearing.

Hit What's Pitched

When it comes to life's disappointments, my dad taught me to "hit what's pitched." This is an admonition coaches give to batters who stand at the plate complaining about how they can't hit the ball unless it's right where they want it. Great hitters "hit what's pitched." Even if it's close to the plate, they go for it. Whether they foul the ball off or get a hit, they make contact. My dad always told us that nobody gets the perfect pitch every time. In life you have to "watch where the ball actually is, not where you hope it will be."

Major-league hitters are a lot like the maturing Christian. Great batters know enough about the pitcher (they listen to scouts and coaches) to anticipate patterns and preferences— how the ball *might* be pitched. But from the time the ball leaves the pitcher's hand till they see the wood on the ball, their eyes don't leave the red-stitched sphere. They look and keep on looking. Sometimes they are sure the pitch will be "low and away," but they sure do move when it's "high and inside"! Wise batters are humble at the plate. Good batters see the pitch as it is, not as they anticipated it—even in good, informed faith.

Recovering from a romantic disappointment can be a hard lesson in learning to "hit what's pitched." It can be more difficult if the disappointment is compounded by a "promise" from God that didn't happen. Taking time to hear the Good Shepherd's voice and clarify his will is invaluable in maturing as an obedient and wise Christian. God's goodness is always better than what we assume is "best" for us. God's will needs to grow larger than our own desire. His will is good. His promises are always kept. And his grace is sufficient to help us learn humbly to "hit what's pitched."

Disappointment After Obedience

Sex on the silver screen is so easy. The guy has shoulders that ripple with passion. The woman has hair that shines even in the dark. Movie stars never seem to wash their faces and actually get ready for bed before they go to bed. Clothes come off without effort or bungling. Intercourse is as smooth as the silk pajamas draped alluringly on a $750 chair. The various sexual positions are adventuresome and never need adjustment. If the phone rings, it's only for a comedy story-line device. No one ever goes to the bathroom, says "Ouch, you're on my arm" or has to sneeze. Except in macho cowboy movies, no one has gas.

Sex isn't the only unrealistic depiction in a Hollywood film. In many movies, people don't even eat. I remember seeing Goldie Hawn and Mel Gibson in one movie go for five days without eating a thing! Generally, beautiful women stay beautiful and handsome men stay handsome. If they sweat, it's attractive and cleaned up by the next scene. Movies are scripted. There are seldom surprises for the actor, director or camera operator. And if something unscripted happens, it ends up as an "outtake," or it's discarded on the cutting-room floor. On a rare occasion everything else is rewritten to make the surprise fit. Movies are manufactured, managed and manipulated to control and contain a certain story. If you see the same movie several times, you know what will happen next.

Real life is not like that. There are surprises in real life—and they don't get to be outtakes. Nothing ends up on the cutting-room floor. Life can be messy sometimes, and it is not rewritten to make everything turn out just right.

Sex is one area where the unpredictable can become the pattern. It can be so good and fun and right and fulfilling! Sex has been a great part of my marriage. I also know that for others it can be one very difficult disappointment.

Anita and Todd

Anita sobbed uncontrollably as she unburdened her heart. She cried to her counselor, "We did everything right, and everything is wrong!" Anita and her husband Todd had both been virgins when they wed. Neither had been sexually abused or had ever experienced anything that would have forewarned them regarding their present dilemma. Out of their understanding of God's Word and their obedience to Christ, they had allowed their physical relationship to keep pace with the degree of their commitment to each other. They had communicated well, spoken the truth in love, guarded against emotional fornication and joyfully anticipated the day they would be husband and wife.

What went wrong? On their honeymoon Anita had found sexual intercourse to be excruciatingly uncomfortable. She had had a gynecological exam prior to her wedding, and although she found it very uncomfortable, the doctor hadn't indicated that anything was wrong. Todd was as thoughtful and careful and gentle as he could be during their attempts to make love. After a few days it was easier to let nonsexual honeymoon activities (sightseeing, shopping, swimming and sports) delay the time of going to bed. Being "too tired" was a comfortable excuse to put off lovemaking attempts. It was frustrating and disappointing for both of them, but they loved each other. They would just work at it, take time, maybe read a few books and not tell anyone. Anita would cry and try harder to make her body receptive. Todd would say, "That's okay, honey; I can wait. I love you."

Sometimes sex isn't easy. It is always awkward at first. I wish I could tell you that Anita and Todd just learned a few helpful hints, read a few books and now are just fine. But I can't, and that's why I decided to include their story in this book. Actually "Anita and Todd" are a composite illustration of several disappointed and frustrated couples who have come to us for help through the years. Most of the Anitas and Todds we have counseled are still married. In varying degrees they still work at sexual comfort and compatibility. Some have arrived at a very satisfying sexual relationship, and others are still on the way. This journey is not easy.

Anita cries in secret every time she hears of someone's enjoyable honeymoon or of a young couple having their first baby. Easy sexual innuendo on TV sitcoms drives Todd out of the room. They don't go to many movies. Every wedding they go to reminds them of how hopeful they had been and how easy they assumed it would all be. They pray for every couple to not have to "hit" their particular "pitch" in the sexual relationship of their marriage. Deep down, Anita and Todd doubt if anyone else has a problem at all.

What went wrong? I don't know. Anita had another examination and follows the doctor's advice on how to maximize her physical ability to have intercourse. Todd is gentle and creative with his lovemaking. Much of his stimulation and ejaculation is outside the vagina, against the body of his wife. When intercourse is possible, the stress makes it exhausting. Anita and Todd love each other and have learned to cope. They have been open to counseling, have prayed fervently and continue to seek the Lord's healing in this part of their relationship.

People don't talk much about sexual disappointment. But it happens. And it happens to wonderful people who have honored the Lord and done everything "right." Anita and Todd are learning to love each other for who they are together. They are two people who are staying in the batter's box and learning to "hit what's pitched." They long for children too.

Sexual disappointment happens to people who could care less about the Lord and did everything "wrong" too. But instead of meeting the challenge of sexual dysfunction together, one partner often leaves the other for an easier relationship. And some people just keep wanting it to happen "like in the movies."

I am very grateful to have an enjoyable and sexually fulfilling relationship with my husband. It has been delightful to learn what is pleasurable for each other and to know each other in an exciting and fully intimate way. Like most couples, we've gotten better with practice. Sex really can be great. Like most couples, we experience sex as much more awkward and human and real than what is portrayed by Hollywood's "perfect" people. In real life, there are no perfect people. And I think that sometimes people like Anita and Todd consider themselves to be the only imperfect people. But they are not alone. I think any book on human sexuality should acknowledge the reality of their special challenge. They are not without hope. And they certainly are not without each other's love.

Gilbert and Frances

Gilbert and Frances are not a composite couple created for this book to keep confidence and hide identities. Gilbert is best known by his initials G. K. He was an Englishman, Christian writer, theologian, philosopher and mentor of the faith in the first part of the twentieth century. Gilbert Keith Chesterton married Frances Blogg in 1901, and they had a six-day honeymoon in England's Norfolk region. Upon their return Gilbert confided to his brother Cecil that all had not gone well. In his biography, *G. K. Chesterton,* Michael Ffinch quotes a diary entry written by Cecil's wife:

> Gilbert felt that . . . his brutality and lust had frightened the woman he would have died to protect. He dared not even contemplate a repetition. . . . Cecil thought that nothing happened that could not be put right . . . but . . . Gilbert hated himself for what had happened.

Ffinch notes in the biography,

> Judging by a letter written in 1924 . . . there was a gynecological reason why [Frances] could not enjoy sexual intercourse; this would explain why Frances . . . underwent an

operation, almost certainly for an imperforate hymen, "to make it possible for her to have children." Unfortunately all attempts to solve the problem proved unsuccessful.

It was a deep source of sadness to both her and Gilbert, for they would dearly have loved to have a family, and Frances ever afterwards felt a sense of failure. But it also bound them more closely together and provided a well of suffering from which they both were able to draw living water, which, with divine grace, enabled them to grow spiritually. Sadly Chesterton wrote five years later:

Oh when the bitter wind of longing blows,
    And all between us seems an aching space
Think that we hold each other close; so close
    We cannot even see each other's face.

From love poems, public praise and the entries of both their private diaries, it is clear that Gilbert and Frances loved each other for a lifetime. They learned in faithfulness, grace and humility to "hit what was pitched."

Even in a Wheelchair

I had a graduate student tell me recently about her struggle to allow God to bring his best into her life. She thought she knew what was best for her, and the fellow she was now dating didn't match her "list." This woman is a full-scholarship collegiate athlete. She runs, pumps iron and wins trophies. She always assumed God's best for her would be a fellow athlete. Surprise! She has discovered the love of her life to be a computer-science whiz who likes to watch sports, not compete in them.

She confessed that in "every other way—especially the ones that really count," this nonathlete was someone she could love. He was a godly man, fully committed to Christ; he was warm, affectionate, thoughtful and attentive. They had a comfortable compatibility and made each other laugh. She told me that through prayer, she had finally surrendered her long-time desire to the Lord's higher and better wisdom. Shortly after that surrender she realized that she would love this man "even in a wheelchair." It struck her forcefully that often great athletes get injured, sometimes drastically and beyond repair. How could her willingness to love someone be so influenced by something so essentially fragile?

This is a good question for all people considering what "true love" really is. Love that is true beyond the shadow of doubt can still be a love with regrets.

Regrets and doubts are different. In the movie *Chariots of Fire* Eric Liddell is remembered as the Olympic runner who refused to compete on a Sunday out of religious conviction. Along with his coach, who is not a believer, Eric attends the final heat of the one-hundred-meter run he very likely would have won had he run in the qualifying race the Sunday before. His coach asks Eric as the runners are lining up at the starting line, "Well, Eric, do you have any regrets?"

Nodding, Eric replies, "Oh, yes—but no doubts!"

Life will always have regrets. Love will have regrets. Marriage will have regrets. The challenge is to live a life without doubts. Doing the right thing doesn't guarantee a life without regret; it does give us the security to live without doubts. Faithfulness isn't a manifestation of feelings, but of the security of a covenant relationship. In this covenant relationship established by God between himself, ourselves and each other, we are no longer alone.

13

True Love . . .
or Not

HOW DO YOU KNOW if you are in love? This is a good question. And all sorts of people want to know the answer—from hyper junior-high kids in the youth group to elderly widowers considering another marriage. Teenagers sometimes ask the question after a first date, and so do grad students starting their fourth year of dating the same person. Movie stars "on location" with Mr. or Ms. Gorgeous and Christians on a summer mission with Mr. or Ms. Person-of-God want to know. Bored couples celebrating another anniversary and passionate couples consummating a date in the back bedroom wonder about the meaning of "true love."

What is true love? Many answers, from "You'll know when you know" to "You never really know," are not too helpful! It is a huge question, and the answer must correspond with the expansiveness of the inquiry. The question is too big and too important for most of us to even attempt to answer. Who can be responsible for such a definition? Whose life can adequately model what the answer is supposed to look like? What is the nature of true love? How do we know if we can give it, receive it, live up to it, fall in it or even recognize it?

What does it mean to be in love? to fall in love? to find true love in a world full of counterfeits? The only adequate and honest answer has to come from someone who accepts responsibility for the answer and reflects its reality in the real world. Who but God is adequate for such a definition and display? Scripture offers both eloquent poetry and practical how-to advice in answering this vital question. Scripture provides a "you are here" reference point as well as a map in our life's journey toward the genuine treasure of true love.

Love Is This and Not That

Lots of brides and grooms want to have 1 Corinthians 13 read at their wedding. It describes the kind of person we would all like to be, and it certainly outlines the kind of person we would all like to marry! Usually we groan with feelings of inadequacy when we read this chapter. We add disclaimers covering personal failure whenever we share the passage with others. Pastors often add anecdotes to sermons on the "Love Chapter" to temper the challenge and the lofty heights of love's definition in the text.

My husband recalls overhearing a casual conversation between a groom and his best man. They were making small talk while waiting to enter the sanctuary, and they were discussing how to get the best service at a restaurant. The groom said, "I talk to the waiter as though I expect to be obeyed." My husband hoped he would not take that condescending attitude into his marriage. It was surely the antithesis of the wedding counseling that both bride and groom had received! The music began, the wedding party entered the sanctuary, and my husband thought he'd better include restaurant etiquette in his advice to those he counseled.

Actually the Love Chapter is Paul's inspired context for deal-

ing with competitiveness and discord in the church family at
Corinth. It's a chapter that inserts a reminder of Eden's ideal
to people squabbling in a distant country over who-gets-what,
who-got-the-most and who's-better-than-whom. Right in the
middle of his "marriage counseling" with the bride of Christ,
Paul says,

> Love is patient, love is kind, and is not jealous; love does not
> brag and is not arrogant, does not act unbecomingly; it does
> not seek its own, is not provoked, does not take into account
> a wrong suffered, does not rejoice in unrighteousness, but
> rejoices with the truth; [love] bears all things, believes all
> things, hopes all things, endures all things. Love never fails.
> (1 Corinthians 13:4–8 NASB)

Many people begin a definition of what it really means to be
in love by a mental list of how that love will meet their needs.
In wedding and marriage counseling more than a few couples
have told Breck and me that they knew it was "true love" when
"she/he made me feel special . . . wonderful . . . appreciated
. . . loved . . . fulfilled . . . complete . . . comfortable . . ." Add
a word that fits a need in your life, and you get the idea.

Marriage can easily become a competition about who gets
their needs met—how well and how quickly. If needs aren't
met, not met well or take too long to be met, "love" is lost, the
marriage is dissatisfying, and divorce is considered a regretta-
ble choice. During premarital counseling my husband asks
couples: "How long do you plan to stay married?" Everyone
always says, "Forever." He responds with another question:
"What do you know about love that makes you think your
marriage will last when so many fail?" Silence usually follows.

The dynamics of two people hoping that their needs can be
met through each other is inherently polarizing. Harvey and
Helen are in love and want to get married. Harvey wants Helen
to meet his needs. Helen wants Harvey to meet her needs.
Harvey and Helen want to be happy. When Helen satisfies Har-

vey, Harvey is happy. When Harvey satisfies Helen, Helen is happy.

Somewhere along the line, often on the honeymoon, Harvey and Helen begin to think that they are getting a little short-changed. Helen has fewer needs met than she seems to be meeting in Harvey's life. She thinks, *It's my turn to be happy, get the attention, be valued, loved.* Harvey wonders when the scales will tip more evenly in his favor. He thinks, *It's my time to be fulfilled, get my way finally, have what I want, be loved.* A competition is established to see who gets their needs met best. As time goes on this competition is increasingly less subtle. Two polarizing points of view are created, and unmet needs, actual or perceived, cause the poles to drift further and further apart. And two dissatisfied people can decide they are not "in love" after all.

Love Is Not a Noun

Paul's challenge to the self-engrossed Corinthians is also great counsel to all Harveys and Helens who want to know what love is really all about. It's not about having your needs met; it's about meeting the needs of another. It's not about being served, but serving. It's not about keeping track; it's about paying the price. It's not about finally getting everything you always wanted; it's about forgiving another for who they cannot be. Love is not a noun—something to have. Love is a verb—something to do.

What does love "do"? God's Word says *love is patient.* The New Testament Greek word *makrothymeō* is derived from a word meaning "great" or "long" and a word meaning "enduring" or "suffering." It means to be generous in waiting, serving and giving someone time and enduring attention. Love is self-restrained and restful in spirit. *Makrothymeō* is a word used to describe God's patience with the human family. It has the sense of being expectant without being in a hurry. It carries the idea of having hopes for one another without imposing your own agenda. In a romantic relationship true love is marked by patience. Love willingly gives people time to become who they are in God's design. Love endures the process because it's good for the one loved. True love is patient.

Love is also kind. This word in Greek carries with it the idea of gentleness in handling something. It includes a respect of usefulness. Kindness wants a person to perform at their best and acts in such a way that the other person is enhanced and not demeaned. Kindness does not harbor a critical spirit or a quick tongue. Kindness is thoughtful and observant. It notices the strengths and gifts of another and creates opportunities for the other person to exercise their attributes. Kindness builds up another person and desires good for them. Love gently enhances the best in another. True love is kind.

Love is not jealous. Jealousy is an inherently competitive attitude. Its root word is the same used for "striving." Jealousy always tries too hard to get what it wants. Love is not this way. It does not "strive" in the sense of stretching itself beyond its means. Jealousy is not conducive to healthy relationships in any way. It wants what it doesn't have or can't have. Jealousy is impatient with time. In jealousy "now" is all that's important, and soon is not soon enough. It is certainly not patient. Jealousy is out for its own good and self-enhancement and in this sense is the opposite of kindness. Love is not spiteful. This plotting meanness is an attitude that comes from jealousy. Spitefulness is selfishness that not only seeks to deny others what is good but also denies itself goodness as part of the cost. True love is not jealous.

Love does not brag. Love is not self-promoting. It does not make itself look better or gain attention at the expense of another. Love does not seek the spotlight. It is not boastful. True love is humble, and so it is surprised by blessing. Love accepts the attentiveness of others, but it does not expect or seek it. People who love well are self-forgetting. Boasting is often based on an insecurity that needs self-assurance. Love that does not brag is based on an assurance that does not need self-propagated security enhancement. The secure person knows that love given is a gift of grace and that love received is cause for humility and awe. Because true love casts out fear (1 John 4:18), there is no need to boast.

Love is not arrogant. This word in the original Greek of Paul's text indicated a person inflated with the pride of their own importance. In the language of the text the tense is passive; the person gets "puffed up." It is part of a prideful vanity that makes the person in the mirror bigger, prettier, handsomer, more efficient, more worthy of honor—more of any desirable quality than is in fact present. When a person is "full of himself," he has no room for loving another. This is the essential problem. To be "puffed up" leaves little room for another's needs and comforts. Love treats the other person as more important and loves the other person as more valuable. True love is not arrogant.

Love does not act unbecomingly. It is not rude. Lovers do not behave disgracefully or dishonorably. True love does not embarrass those loved. There is a think–ahead thoughtfulness that marks how we love another person. Love that is not rude is a love that is considerate and courteous. It is an attitude that speaks the truth in love—at the right time and in the right way. Love does not jest at another person's expense. True lovers guard the public life of those they love. One of the most important things Breck and I urge couples to make habitual in their relationship is honest public praise. It's one thing to appreciate another's attribute in private ("Pat, that was a great meal." "Thanks for fixing the sink. You're wonderful, Sandy!"). It is something altogether endearing to appreciate another person in front of other people ("Pat is a good cook. Our meal the other night was terrific." "Sandy is so handy. If it's broken, it'll get fixed!"). True love is gracious, not rude.

Love does not insist on its own way. Love, as rendered literally from the Greek text, "does not seek the things of herself." Love isn't out for its own sake, its own agenda, its own welfare or its own ends. True love is the opposite of self-seeking and self-serving. Love seeks the welfare of the other, and searches for a way to serve and not be served. Love adopts the agenda that is best for the other person. Love gives way to the needs of the one loved. It does not push for its own accommodation, but creates a comfort zone for the other's life. True love is not insistent, except in its persistence to love the other.

Love is not provoked. Another English word derived from the Greek word used by Paul is often used in the field of medicine. *Paroxysm* is a sudden stopping and starting of a heart rhythm or the sudden cramping and uncramping of a muscle. Paroxysmal activity is unpredictable. It gives no warning when it begins or ends. In the original text the Greek word is passive, meaning it carries the sense of having a "life of its own." Being provoked means to be irritated and touchy. It is associated with sudden fits of temper and anger. This kind of attitude creates an atmosphere described by the idiom "walking on eggshells." True love does not engender such tension. True love puts others at ease. It is in many respects so dependable that others *know* what to expect.

True love can be spontaneous but not sudden. Spontaneity is in accord with a person's values and temperament—only the timing or the setting is a surprise. In a truly loving relationship the intention is always a pleasant surprise. Suddenness comes from a lack of thoughtfulness or consistency. Suddenness breeds insecurity and robs a relationship of rest and joy. Love is not exasperated and undependable. Love is not provoked, paroxysmal. True love is like a steady heartbeat and a strong muscle.

Love does not take into account a wrong suffered. Love does not keep track of wrongdoing. In Greek, the word translated "take into account" was often used as an accounting and legal term. Love does "not reckon the evil." It does not pull out the ledger of life and record what went wrong. Love does not store up memories of being shortchanged, wronged, sinned against or misunderstood. True love does not store up ammunition to be used in the next dispute. Love does not drag up stuff from three years, weeks or days ago to make a point, win an argument or remind another person how she or he has failed. True love is not resentful.

Love does not rejoice at wrong, but rejoices in the truth. Love celebrates the other person. Lovers are each other's best cheerleaders. Win, lose or draw, the loved one is the one you cheer for. True love does not grow from fair-weather friendships. There is a stick-to-itiveness in true love. And when things go right, especially after hard work and long seasons of effort, there is joy. Love, in the same way, shares the pain of disappointment and failure with the one loved. It hurts to see someone you love lose—even when they might have done things differently. Love supports the ideas and plans and enthusiasm of the other person even when personal interest is at a minimum. For instance, my love listens to Breck's enthusiasm for roller-coaster-induced sensations even when Ferris wheels are a challenge to me. Love is glad for the other person's joy, even when it is a foreign experience. True love rejoices in the right.

Love bears all things. The idea here is that love can "cover anything." The Greek word translated "bear" was used to indicate something designed to "hold out" or "hold in" something else. It was associated with the idea of a protective covering. Love like this endures patiently the ups and downs of life. It faces disappointment without panic. "Love covers over a multitude of sins" (1 Peter 4:8). Love like this provides protection from the storms of life. Lovers offer an acceptance that provides an emotional covering from the criticism and harshness of others. Love is not blind, but it does conceal what is displeasing in another. Love does not publicly criticize the other person. Love protects what is vulnerable in the loved person from all that might be wounding. True love bears all things.

Love believes all things and hopes all things. Love is *for* the other person. In Greek, the root word for "believe" is the same root for the word *faith*. True love responds in faith to the character and intention of the one loved. Again, love is not blind, but love sees the best possible in another. Love supports and encourages the dreams and efforts of the loved one. Love places confidence in the know-how of the one loved. Love believes when doubt is a threat. And love hopes at the same time. Love wants the best, and watches for the best. Hope is an assurance of unseen things. Love that hopes is love that watches for love even when it is unseen. Love continues to hope when disappointment is a reality. True love believes and hopes.

And love endures all things. The key Greek word here is *hypomenō.* It literally reflects the word for "under" and the word for "wait" or "abide." Love that endures is a love that stays put. It is a love that is immovable. True love endures until it is victorious. It does not give up. It overcomes and is not overwhelmed. Love like this lasts because it does not entertain another option. The only kind of prenuptial agreement for this kind of love is to work at it for a lifetime. True love endures.

Love like this never fails. Whether in friendship or romance, love is serving the other person. It's doing what is good for them. It is wanting the best for them. This love kneels with Jesus at the dusty feet of tired and needy people and does what needs to be done. This love does not fail because it bows, instead of brags. This love does not fail because it is not trying to succeed, but to serve. True love will not fail.

Love like this is God's intention for all human relationships—not just romance and marriage. It always has been. We are a long way from Eden. But we can edge our way in the right direction. That's how true love is learned—along the way. Patiently, kindly, without spite or self-promotion, without pride and with grace, not irritably or resentfully, but with joy in what goes right—every inch closer to "home," bearing, believing, hoping and enduring all things.

Relational Homelessness

Considering what love really means is pretty intimidating for sinful people. Who can ever "get it right"? No wonder many people say, "I'll never get married!" Who has ever seen love like this from another human perfectly displayed? Many think is it better to keep a safe distance from even trying to love another person like this. Surely we will fail. Yes, we will. But we can get better and better.

The chapter introducing this book is titled "Edging Toward Eden." It reflects the reality of how much we have to learn about who we are supposed to be in relationships with others. It acknowledges that we only make baby steps of progress day by day. Loving like this is hard for those cast out of Eden. Relationships have been corrupted to the core from the rebellion by the "apple" tree. Like our parents in Eden, we wanted to be like God and instead found ourselves less truly human. The consequence was an estrangement from God, others and even ourselves.

Relational homelessness plagues our lives. So it is tempting to wander from person to person or settle for an emotional "cardboard box" just big enough for one. Both options are lonely and don't help us make our way back where we belong. Whether it's in Eden or out, God said it is not good for us to be alone. We need to learn to love, edging our way back to where we belong. And it will take a lifetime to learn. This is why marriage, as a lifelong relationship, is so valuable. A lifelong marriage is a safe haven for relationally homeless people to live and learn and love. Marriage is one of God's best discipling tools. It provides a place to learn to love and a person to practice with.

Love Is a Verb

In 1 Corinthians 13 we have seen how God defines love. This is the definition of love, the pattern for true love. So how does this love look in the marriage relationship? Scripture provides a picture of this kind of married love in Ephesians 5:21–33. The sentence that begins this section actually starts in verse 18. God's Word admonishes us to be controlled by the Holy Spirit and not anything else (v. 18), to speak and sing to one another in fellowship and to God in worship (v. 19) and always to give thanks to God for everything (v. 20).

In the context of Spirit-controlled and Scripture-enriched relationships, full of worship and gratitude, God defines love as being subject to one another "out of reverence for Christ" (v. 21). From there the Word describes how this love is to look in marriage. This first snapshot of married love pictures two servants in mutual submission for the other's welfare because this is how Christ Jesus has treated them. Lovers are servants. Love is service.

In John 13, after Jesus washed the feet of his disciples, he asked, "Do you understand what I have done for you?" Of course they knew that their rabbi and master had done the work of the lowliest house servant to refresh them in bathing their feet. Jesus asked the question to make sure they saw in his action a model for their own lives. Jesus explained,

> You call me "Teacher" and "Lord," and rightly so, for that is what I am. Now that I, your Lord and Teacher, have washed your feet, you also should wash one another's feet. I have set you an example that you should do as I have done for you. (John 13:13-15)

In Ephesians 5 we are reminded that this is the basic posture of love in human relationships. If we love each other, we are to serve each other. In the married relationship, Paul provides women with the right attitude for this mutual submission, and he provides men with the right action for this mutual submission.

Using the verb *submit* from verse 21, Paul addresses women first: "wives, to your husbands as to the Lord" (v. 22—note that the Greek does not repeat the verb as most English translations do). In the first century there was nothing new or startling about a wife's subjection to her husband; it was presumed. But Paul wants the Christian woman to have a new attitude about her place as a helpmate and fellow servant. The love that a wife shows to her husband by serving him reflects her love and devotion to Jesus Christ. In this way, Scripture contributes to the redemptive nature of a wife's position by giving it value and meaning beyond the immediate benefit of the service rendered. Because the woman has had her "feet washed" by the Lord, she follows this example in "washing the feet" of her husband. Because she is served, she serves. Because she is loved, she loves.

There is a tendency, to say the least, for women to see in this text the creation of a second-class status for wives. But we must remember that *all* servants are second-class. We are *all* to be subject to one another; it is not an oppressive or unequal relationship.

In this passage Paul is telling us how to untangle the relational knots created by the rebellion in Eden and summarized by God in Genesis 3:16. The "rule" of one over the other is a consequence of sin, not a model for how things were meant to be.

In Paul's lengthy command to husbands in Ephesians 5, we see a model much closer to what God intended. The way a husband serves is in loving his wife (v. 25). He is to do this as Christ loves the church—by functioning as the "head" in the relationship (v. 23). The Greek word in this passage, often translated into English as "head," is *kephalē*. The same word is used to describe Christ himself as head of the church; he is the source, the fountainhead and the fullness of everything (Ephesians 1:20–23; 4:15; Colossians 1:18; 2:10; 2:19). So the husband's headship does not so much imply superiority or hierarchical authority as much as it implies being, through Christ, the source of satisfaction in the married relationship.*

This posture alone can protect the wife in her vulnerability as a servant. But Paul continues. He adds that a husband is to love his wife without limit—even to the point of giving up his own life for her! Why? Because "Christ loved the church and gave himself up for her" (v. 25). This kind of love from a husband is given for the spiritual (vv. 26–27), physical (vv. 28–30) and social (v. 31) welfare of his wife. In the first century this was revolutionary! It still is.

Today people of God need to be a part of revolutionizing both aspects of the teaching in Ephesians 5. We can only speculate as to the riches that have been lost on both sides of Paul's metaphor. A marriage based on unilateral superiority and unilateral submission creates an impotence of love that renders

---

*In Greek lexicons, including those which consider Homeric, classical Greek and the "common" or Koine Greek of the New Testament, and covering the language from about 1000 B.C. to A.D. 600 there are less than ten instances when the use for *kephalē* would indicate inherent authority or superiority. In the Old Testament, as translated into the Greek Septuagint, there are only two passages where *kephalē* implies authority or superior rank. However, there are 180 times when a Hebrew word denoting authority is translated into the Greek using not *kephalē* but another Greek word, *archōn*. *Archōn* is the Greek word of choice when hierarchical authority or superiority is meant. This indicates that *kephalē* as "head" has a different meaning. The distinction is important because in the inspiration of Scripture the choice of *kephalē* to convey the idea of headship for husbands is purposeful and informative. (In addition to my own word study, I found the work of Berkeley and Alvera Mickelsen, "The Head of the Epistles," *Christianity Today*, February 1981, a helpful summary.)

a relationship sterile and dissatisfying. Feelings of vulnerability lead to incompatibility. Christian women and men considering dating and marriage need to depolarize the meet-my-needs competition that defines relationships in our culture today. We must look at our feet, washed by the Lord Jesus, and follow his example of love in how we seek to serve one another. As we submit to one another, our independent barrenness gives way to a fruitful life of love and mutual purpose.

If husbands and wives are not mutually loving servants, their marriage dissolves into a competition of cohabiters without patience or kindness, full of jealousy, arrogance, insensitivity, selfishness and resentment. Instead of sharing joy, faith, hope and fortitude for the long haul, marriages fail.

What does love look like? It looks like a servant looking for ways to meet the needs of a fellow servant as if that servant owned the estate! How do you recognize true love in a world of false hopes? What does it mean to be in love? It means a willingness to bring love as service to a special and exclusive relationship. How do you know when you are in love? When you are willing to give a lifetime to someone learning together how to get it right. Love never fails . . . to serve.

Epilogue:

Redeemed Rebels

In our journey home to Eden, we do come to a Grand Canyon that must be crossed. Sexual holiness is important for a godly relationship between a man and a woman. Bridges built for crossing need to have guardrails if any sort of freedom, as well as safety, is to be experienced in the adventure. I hope this book has offered you some trustworthy guardrails. And I hope the canyon is more grand and more beautiful than you thought it might be. I hope you are less fearful and more wise.

I believe that Chesterton's reflection quoted in the introduction of this book—"in this world heaven is rebelling against hell"—is quite true. Redeemed rebels are called to a righteousness that exceeds the simple rule-keeping of Pharisees or the talk-show opinions of modern religious scribes. We are far from Eden, but every step closer is good. Every step closer honors our waiting and watchful Father. Every step closer says who we really are as those redeemed by the blood of Jesus. Every step closer to Eden gives evidence in the middle of the journey that God's Spirit is in the world still. Learning to love truly makes us truly human.

In his book *The God Who Is There,* Francis Schaeffer accurately summarizes the mark of the Christian: "Christians in their relationships should be the most *human* people you will ever see. This speaks for God in an age of inhumanity and impersonality and facelessness."

I admit that Breck and I have a marriage that many hope for but too few have ever seen. Some want to tell us that our relationship is rare, but we are quick to assert that this should not be the case for kingdom people. We acknowledge that our love, truthfully reflected in the pages of this book, may seem to some a "false hope." It is not. We haven't always *done* what's right, but from the beginning we *knew* what was right. Because of this, we've continued to head in the right direction.

We have worked hard to learn each other's "love language." Breck and I have had to confess our faults to one another—staying up very late sometimes so that the sun wouldn't go down on our anger. We have disappointed each other along the way and have been the source of each other's regrets on occasion. Breck may never find it easy to give me the encouragement I need. I may never slow my pace to match Breck's calm stride through life. But we work at it. Marriage has made us more human. We have no doubts that our love is for a lifetime, and we guard this treasure with attention and prayer.

Breck and I are also grateful to have had role models for healthy marriages that many others lack. Our parents were mutual servants and exercised "love as a verb." In our early days of courtship and young marriage, we had a few friends who invited us to take a close look at their maturing marriages. I hope that this book offers some encouragement and pictures of real people that can help you believe that true love is possible in a world of few role models, let alone false hopes.

True Love in a World of False Hope has been a labor of thanksgiving for my married life. As you consider the possibilities of lifelong love for yourself, I pray that God's answer will be as grand as his gift of love to me. In my marriage I really can say with Paul, "I would to God, that whether in a short or long time . . . [you] might become as I am." I hope your journey toward Eden will be helped by what I've shared. Journey well. And remember: KYEOJ.